Studying Complex Interactions and Outcomes Through Qualitative Comparative Analysis

Studying Complex Interactions and Outcomes Through Qualitative Comparative Analysis: A Practical Guide to Comparative Case Studies and Ethnographic Data Analysis offers practical, methodological, and theoretically robust guidelines to systematically study the causalities, dynamics, and outcomes of complex social interactions in multiple source data sets. It demonstrates how to convert data from multisited ethnography of investment politics, mobilizations, and citizen struggles into a Qualitative Comparative Analysis (QCA).

In this book, Markus Kröger focuses on how data collected primarily via multisited political ethnography, supplemented by other materials and verified by multiple forms of triangulation, can be systematically analyzed through QCA. The results of this QCA offer insight on how to study the political and economic outcomes in natural resource conflicts across different contexts and political systems. This book applies the method in practice using examples from the author's own research. With a focus on social movement studies, it shows how QCA can be used to analyze a multiple data source database that includes results from multiple case studies.

This book is a practical guide for researchers and students in social movement studies and other disciplines that produce ethnographic data from multiple sources on how to analyze complex databases through the QCA.

Markus Kröger is Associate Professor in Global Development Studies at the University of Helsinki, Finland, and an Academy of Finland Research Fellow. He is a founding member of the Global Extractivisms and Alternatives Initiative (EXALT). His research interests include Brazilian studies, global natural resource politics, and social movement strategies and economic outcomes.

Studying Complex Interactions and Outcomes Through Qualitative Comparative Analysis

A Practical Guide to Comparative Case Studies and Ethnographic Data Analysis

Markus Kröger

LONDON AND NEW YORK

First published 2021
by Routledge
2 Park Square, Milton Park, Abingdon, Oxon OX14 4RN

and by Routledge
605 Third Avenue, New York, NY 10158

Routledge is an imprint of the Taylor & Francis Group, an informa business

© 2021 Markus Kröger

The right of Markus Kröger to be identified as author of this work has been asserted by him in accordance with sections 77 and 78 of the Copyright, Designs and Patents Act 1988.

All rights reserved. No part of this book may be reprinted or reproduced or utilised in any form or by any electronic, mechanical, or other means, now known or hereafter invented, including photocopying and recording, or in any information storage or retrieval system, without permission in writing from the publishers.

Trademark notice: Product or corporate names may be trademarks or registered trademarks, and are used only for identification and explanation without intent to infringe.

British Library Cataloguing-in-Publication Data
A catalogue record for this book is available from the British Library

Library of Congress Cataloging-in-Publication Data
A catalog record for this book has been requested

ISBN: 978-0-367-55780-5 (hbk)
ISBN: 978-1-032-03920-6 (pbk)
ISBN: 978-1-003-09510-1 (ebk)

Typeset in Times New Roman
by Apex CoVantage, LLC

Contents

List of maps	vi
List of tables	vii
Acknowledgments	viii
List of abbreviations	xi
Introduction	1
1 Systematic data collection and analysis: multi-sited political ethnography, QCA, and other methods for assessing complex causalities	9
2 Studying complex interactions and outcomes: selecting key factors in social movement studies	33
3 How to apply QCA? An illustration through a QCA of investment politics outcomes in Brazil and India	50
4 Complementing QCA by a detailed opening of explanatory factors	94
Conclusions	117
References	125
Index	134

Maps

1.1 Displays the major iron ore mining project areas of India between 2005 and 2015, which I studied. The bounded geographical areas on the map are different sizes, referring to the approximate extensions of the mining case area.   25
1.2 Presents the main iron ore extraction areas of Brazil that are discussed herein.   26

Tables

1.1	Disaggregation of processes into mechanisms and strategies in extractive politics: activeness observation protocols	22
3.1	Cases studied, location, case type, main companies, and main resistance groups	51
3.2	QCA summary of findings on movement strategies	55
3.3	Legend of abbreviations used in the QCA tables	56
3.4	Cases where all mines or projects were discontinued (before 2015)	58
3.5	Peaceful resistance by the concatenated use of all strategies a–e	66
3.6	Armed revolutionary agency and resistance outcomes	68
3.7	Contextual factors and contingencies in Indian and Brazilian iron mining politics	71
3.8	Legend for the contingencies in Indian and Brazilian mining politics	72
3.9	The role of third parties	76
3.10	Underestimation of resistance potential by the targets (CD1)	78
3.11	Resistance targeting smaller companies (CD2 = 0)	79
3.12	Corporate countertactics to curb mobilization (CD3)	80
3.13	QCA truth table on necessary resistance strategies in non–civil war India, with logical remainders	83
3.14	QCA truth table on necessary resistance strategies in non–civil war India	85
3.15	Exploring for alternative explanations of investment outcomes through QCA	87
3.16	Recalibrated values for the Minas-Rio case (2005–2015) based on new information obtained in 2020	90

Acknowledgments

Funding for the research that contributed to this book was provided via the following grants:

1. The Kone Foundation postdoctoral fellow project, "Contentious Agency and Corporate Resource Exploitation: A Qualitative Comparative Analysis on Social Movement Impacts on Paper and Steel Industry in Brazil and India";
2. The Academy of Finland project, "The Politics of Corporate Resource Exploitation: Social Movement Influence on Paper and Metal Industry Investments in Brazil and India" (grant number 251321, postdoctoral fellow project);
3. The Academy of Finland project, "Human Ecology, Land Conversion and the Global Resource Economy" (grant number 253680); and
4. The Academy of Finland project, "Political economies of deforestation: The impact of regionally dominant resource sectors in the forest politics of Brazil, Peru and Finland."

I appreciate the Academy of Finland and the Kone Foundation for the financial support that made this book possible.

The scope and scale of the research that contributed to this book required support and assistance from many people. I have been helped in numerous ways during the course of this multiyear project, and I am especially indebted to the hundreds of informants in Brazil and India who shared their time and expertise with me. This assistance ranged from sitting for interviews (and walking in forests and mining sites with me), connecting me with new sites, and helping me with the many logistics of conducting fieldwork.

There are some individuals who went above and beyond and who deserve specific mention. In Maranhão, Brazil, I owe thanks to Divina, Regina, José Luis, Antonio, and all the others who made it possible for me to do my fieldwork. In Pará, special thanks go to Ulisses Manacas, Adima, Leticia, Maria Raimunda, Gabriela, Cassia, Salete, Claudio Ferreira, and Pablo Carrasco for kindly hosting me and/or providing logistical assistance. Among many others in the other parts of Brazil, I am indebted to Pertti Simula, Biancca Castro, Mariana Penna, Rodrigo Santos, Carlos Bittencourt, Maria Gomes, Felício Pontes, and José Batista for their help and insightful commentaries.

In India, I am extremely grateful to Sebastian Rodrigues and all the others who helped me in Goa; to Leo Saldanha and others in Karnataka; to Piyush Manush in Tamil Nadu; and to Rabi Pradhan and Duskar Barik, in Odisha, Chhattisgarh, New Delhi, and Jharkhand, as well as many others, who selflessly provided crucial help.

One of the most important aspects of putting together large-scale research projects is the discussion and constructive criticism of colleagues; in this regard, thank you to Ville-Veikko Hirvelä, Kai Vaara, Satu Ranta-Tyrkkö, Juho Partanen, Pekka Pennanen, Bobby Banerjee, Carlos Santana, Samarendra Das, Felix Padel, Eduardo Gudynas, Heather Bedi, Anita Basu, Subash Mohapatra, and Sam Agarwal.

I have had the honor and opportunity to work on the ideas for this book and the research that served as my examples at many conferences where I have received helpful peer review, comments, and discussions. I am grateful to Jun Borras, Alberto Fradejas, Tania Li, Larry Lohmann, Joan Martinez Alier, Natalia Mamonova, Ben McKay, Sara Mingorría, and Henry Bernstein for discussions on many different occasions, including the different Food Sovereignty and International Critical Agrarian Studies conferences organized by the International Institute of Social Studies. I extend thanks to my fellow panelists from the Brazilian Studies Association: Kathryn Hochstetler, Andréa Zhouri, Klemens Laschefski, and Marcos Pedlowski. During the World-Ecology Research Network conferences, I appreciate constructive discussions with Jason W. Moore, Ossi Ollinaho, Joshua Eichen, Andrew Pragacz, and Marcus Taylor, among many others. For the feedback I received at the International Studies Association panels, I owe thanks to Amy Below, Vinicius Rodrigues, Marieke de Hoon, Mark Axelrod, Surupa Gupta, and Moises Arce. During an International Rural Studies Association conference, I shared a productive panel on mining with Jo-Anne Everingham and Sandra Franco. I have had many fruitful discussions during the International Sociological Association conferences with Peter Evans and James Goodman. I am grateful to comments by Adriana Margutti, Gustavo Oliveira, Sérgio Sauer, and others during the BRICS Agrarian Studies conferences. Finally, from during the many development days conferences held in Helsinki, I have had constructive comments from Neera Chandroke and Dinah Rajak, among many others.

My colleagues in Finland have also been very helpful, from commenting, to proofing, to editing. From Global Development Studies, at the University of Helsinki, I want to thank Barry Gills, Anja Nygren, Franklin Obeng-Odoom, Maria Ehrnström-Fuentes, and Gutu Wayessa; from World Politics and Political Science, Teivo Teivainen, Pertti Ahonen, Jussi Pakkasvirta, and Juri Mykkänen; and from Anthropology, Timo Kaartinen and Sarah Green.

This book was improved and refined through the careful edits and comments especially from Sophia Hagolani-Albov and also from Saana Hokkanen, Nely Keinänen, Marie-Louise Karttunen, and Sanna Komi. In addition, I received useful developmental commentaries from Audra Wolfe and Tara Mendola. I am also deeply grateful for important last-minute comments on the book by Charles Ragin and Benoît Rihoux.

Last, but certainly not least, I appreciate the support and assistance of my wife, Jenni Munne, in so many facets of this research.

Abbreviations

a	Organizing and politicizing a mass social movement, local middle classes largely supported resistance
a2	Key resistance group included urban, middle-class professionals in key positions
a3	Several cross-class, interethnic, or intersector resistance groups
b	Campaigning by heterodox, nonmodernist, anti-mining framing in Brazil, Russia, India, China, and South Africa
bt	billion tons
c	Physically nonviolent protesting that is noted
CD1	Underestimation of the resistance potential by the targets
CD2	Size of the company(ies): 1 = large, 0 = small
CD3	Sophisticated corporate countertactics to curb mobilization
csQCA	Crisp-set Qualitative Comparative Analysis
CSR	Corporate social responsibility
d	Networking with other resistance groups
e1	Embedding electoral politics, for example, via targeted voting of politicians opposing mining or allying with politicians seeking mine closure while retaining movement autonomy
e2	Embedding institutional politics, for example, by acquiring progressive state-actor-led investigations via advocacy, successfully demanding regulatory institutions to intervene to uphold the rule of law, occupying key institutions, or crafting new institutions while maintaining autonomy
e3	Embedding judicial politics that helps the resistance in litigation in court against the project while retaining autonomy
EJOLT	Environmental Justice Organizations, Liabilities and Trade
EO1	All mines (and/or all projects) discontinued
EO2	Some mines closed, expansion extension and volume significantly curtailed, and/or very major impact

	on extraction style (e.g., nonmechanized, worker-controlled mine)
EO3	Expansion decelerated
f	Participation in private politics initiatives of companies (CSR, etc.) where an agreement is reached
Fiocruz	The Oswaldo Cruz Foundation
fsQCA	Fuzzy-set Qualitative Comparative Analysis
g1	Armed revolutionary resistance used
g2	Threat of resistance by arms is explicit, but no violence takes place
GDP	Gross domestic product
GE1	High-quality ore (over 60% average iron content)
HNF	HOTnHIT News features
MAB	Movement of People Affected by Dams
MAM	Movement for Popular Sovereignty over Mining
MOU	Memoranda of understanding
MST	Brazilian Landless Rural Workers' Movement
mt	million tons
mvQCA	Multi-value Qualitative Comparative Analysis
NACAB	Nucleus of Assistance to Communities Affected by Dams
NGO	Nongovernmental organization
P1	Primarily central-government-led expansion
P2	A primary national resource frontier
P3	A deep ethnic injustice: mining that represents a profound, ethnic injustice by primarily benefiting elite ethnic groups and perpetrating forestland loss that mostly affects vulnerable communities (e.g., indigenous groups)
PO1	Transnational spread of resistance
PO2	National spread of political and economic outcomes from this locality
PO3	Locally enduring, strong resistance capacities and willingness created
PO4	Armed revolutionary agency created and spread across states by the conflict experience of the resistance
PPP	Public Private Partnerships
QCA	Qualitative Comparative Analysis
REAJA	Rede de Articulacao e Justica dos Atingidos do Projeto Minas-Rio, the Network of Articulation and Justice of People Affected by the Minas-Rio Project
SAIL	Steel Authority of India Limited

SLO	Social License to Operate
T1	Tourism, agriculture, or other significant mining-critical industries present
T2	Ore went or would go primarily to China
TSM	Towards Sustainable Mining

Introduction

Book abstract: *This book is a practical guidebook on how to apply the method of Qualitative Comparative Analysis (QCA). The popularity of QCA has been rising rapidly as a method to explain complex causalities and conduct systematic comparisons. This book provides insight into the process of QCA through an exploration of concrete cases of social conflicts and politics and illustrates in practice how QCA can be utilized for research that addresses important real-world topics. The focus of this book is to showcase how data collected primarily via multi-sited, political ethnography, when supplemented by other materials and verified by multiple forms of triangulation, can be systematically analyzed through QCA. The results of QCA offer insights into how to study the political and economic outcomes in political ecological conflicts across different contexts and political systems. To illustrate the use of this analytical method, I draw on the findings from two large research projects that compare the political dynamics across mining and forestry areas and projects in Brazil and India.*

Chapter abstract: *This chapter introduces the book as a hands-on guide addressing the practical application of systematic comparative methods for ethnographic data generated through social movement studies and research into other complex phenomena. This chapter explores the novelty, importance, and contribution of this book. While there are other books on Qualitative Comparative Analysis (QCA), this contribution offers a usable and unique hands-on, practical approach that offers easily accessible guidance to a complex analytical method. The book is anchored in social movement outcomes, ethnographic data, and QCA; however, most of the attention is focused on showing how complex interactions and outcomes can be assessed in other, policy-relevant research.*

Introducing QCA

When I started my own research, I could not find books that offered advice on using Qualitative Comparative Analysis (QCA) methods with multi-sited ethnographic data. Some book chapters or articles tangentially addressed the QCA methodology, sometimes even in conjunction with social movement studies, but they did not provide a longer exposition on how to apply the method in practice. Part of my motivation for writing this guidebook was to save other researchers some of the potential frustrations and pitfalls of figuring out aspects of the practical use of this method. QCA has proved useful in my own work, and I want to provide insight into how to successfully apply it. I am not alone in this desire, as Wagemann (2014) also called for more QCA-based studies on social movement outcomes, which is what I will specifically address in this book.

QCA was first introduced by Charles Ragin (1987). This method is based on a long tradition of comparative analysis that systematically tries to make sense of a very complex world. One of the cornerstones behind the development of this kind of systematic thinking on causalities in social sciences is the world-systems analysis of Immanuel Wallerstein (1974). Political science and sociology are among the key disciplines utilizing the method; however, use of QCA has also proliferated among scholars of other social and environmental sciences, including management and health. The utilization of QCA has also expanded to development studies and many other more policy-focused fields. One of the key reasons for this proliferation is that the method allows researchers to draw causal inferences based on configurational data and the assistance of Boolean minimization (where supposed explanatory factors and dependent variables are marked by a binary logic as either active or inactive, with a 1 or 0, respectively) (Baumgartner and Thiem 2020). Although QCA has some of its logical and epistemological roots in the methodological logic of David Hume and Karl Popper, it is difficult—if not impossible—to fulfill the positivist dream of proving a causal path or a hypothesis as definitively true through this (or other) social scientific method (Berg-Schlosser et al. 2009).[1] Instead, QCA serves best as a tool to eliminate causal conditions, rather than to confirm them (Ragin 1987, 2014). The focus in QCA is on eliminating irrelevant factors and false hypotheses, through systematic comparisons, by means of a logic where different hypotheses and causal paths are compared. This elimination is based on intimacy with the studied phenomena, which allows the researcher to have a greater basis for validating what is going on in the cases (i.e., what are the configurations and causalities that matter and which conditions can be eliminated, after proper consideration and multiple rounds of QCA).

Before QCA can be conducted, one needs to be well-versed in the particulars and details of the cases one is comparing, or at least several of them, as QCA works best when used with substantive knowledge of cases (Ragin 2014, 2019). Some of the cases within the case set for QCA can be less well-known to the researcher and are included for the sake of having databases that contain all the relevant cases. However, before the end of the research process, these cases should also be explored in detail. There is still much need for developing QCA applications along these lines, making cases better known, and thus better exploiting QCA (Gerrits and Pagliarin 2020). Knowledge of each case inside and out is extremely important for the reliability of QCA results, as each case matters in QCA; this stands as one of the important factors that differentiates the technique from statistical methods. In case-study-based research, one gains this familiarity through the process of gathering data, especially in case approaches relying on field research, which includes interviews, participant observation, and ethnography. Typically, the researchers who know their cases best, for example, anthropologists, are those who produce "thick descriptions" and often spend a year or more exploring a particular place or topic with a focus on ethnographic inquiry and understanding all its complexities and mechanisms. These researchers would not make use of QCA or related configurational comparison techniques. However, in some cases there is a need and an argument for using QCA within these research fields. This method is useful for uniting several case studies carried out by other researchers with one's own multi-sited ethnography. The QCA allows the researcher to confront the thick descriptions with new data and conjectures. Scholars of comparative methods have called for this kind of methodological opening (Berg-Schlosser et al. 2009).

For this reason, in this book I suggest ways for ethnographers and others using field research—through which very complex real-world events and causalities can be observed—to make wider use of QCA as a tool to analyze the rich case data collected. Multi-sited ethnography and political ethnography are budding fields of ethnographically oriented research, which observe how processes unfold in different contexts in time and place and how power and politics manifest, respectively. I explain how one can use a merger of these approaches to explore how the politics around a certain topic at a certain time unfold in different places during a given period. QCA is used as a lens to look for possible modest generalizations (not broad, as in statistics) and specifications that can be inferred from the comparison of the cases. This kind of comparison is a type of incorporated comparison (McMichael 2000), in that it explores how different instances form a whole. This type of incorporated comparison can be made more systematic and precise by using the QCA method, which is by design complexity oriented. The QCA method begins at the assumption that everything matters and then simplifies (Vaisey 2014). Yet, it is a useful method for the analytical task of simplifying the overt complexity of social life that is encountered in ethnographic data collection. The data explored through QCA can help when generating hypotheses about the type of causalities that might be present or when identifying the key phenomena in an ever-changing world, which warrant the researcher's attention.

Typically, the goal of QCA is to find a minimal causal combination that explains the phenomenon that one is studying. However, QCA can also be used for many other purposes, such as organizing and rethinking through the multiple cases one is comparing, multi-sited ethnographic material, or other complex datasets that require systematic analysis. Even if one cannot find a direct minimal causal combination, the tables produced through the QCA are helpful for organizing the analysis and write-up of complex phenomena. de Block and Vis (2019) offer practical and general advice on how one should start using QCA when having multiple types of data sources, including how to use qualitative evidence through different kinds of QCA applications. In ethnography, the data analyzed are typically nonnumerical, which is why crisp-set QCA (csQCA) or multi-value QCA (mvQCA) is also useful (for reasons why to use mvQCA, see Cronqvist and Berg-Schlosser 2009). In csQCA, the value given to the conditions follows Boolean logic and is designated either 1 or 0 (denoting that the causal condition is either active or inactive, or that the given outcome is present or not, respectively), while in mvQCA one can assign round values beyond just 0 or 1, for example, 2, 3, 9, or 48. Such a number could be used to denote many different things, for example, the number of times a protest event was noted by the press. I have used both these methods in combination with complex ethnographic data. If one has good, reliable, statistical data available for the topic under investigation, and if one believes these statistical data are best for explaining the phenomena that need to be explained, then one could use fuzzy-set QCA (fsQCA). In fsQCA, one can assign more precise, interval values, that is, membership scores can range from 0 to 1. For example, one can have a four-value fuzzy set (0, 0.33, 0.67, and 1 as membership scores), and the thresholds for these can be based on qualitative or statistical assessments or some other criteria. However, if one is using statistical data, instead of ethnographically attained, process-tracing-based data, then one must be careful not to overextend the claims of causality. This is because in the process-tracing-based data, careful attention has been given to finding and understanding the causal relations in order to create the explanatory factors, conditions, and outcomes based on this cultivated understanding. The detail given to studying the phenomena in question gives csQCA, when based on ethnographic material without nonobserved cases, a much stronger footing in arguing for causal paths. However, linkage of numerical differences to causal claims is tricky and generally should be avoided, for example, when deriving causal claims from measures calculated by someone else like gross domestic product (GDP) per capita and a country's governance indicator. Correlations and possible relations can be detected, but derivation of actual and defensible causal paths from this type of data is difficult. When one makes causal claims, they should be backed as much as possible by ethnographic and process-tracing analysis, which supplements the core structure of arguments provided via QCA truth tables. In this handbook, one will learn these procedures through an in-depth look at my experiences using QCA. I will show how to conduct QCA across complex cases and how to supplement the analysis with ethnographic descriptions and analysis, which first identifies and then assesses the possible causalities. I will also introduce a form of QCA that focuses on the probabilistic analysis of interactions, instead of seeking primarily minimal formulas, and explain when, how, and why this form of analysis is useful and even preferable.

A specific section is dedicated to demonstrating how and why QCA analysts can and should open up the process of doing research and how to recalibrate their findings. In this section, I also discuss how it is possible to perform data triangulation in situations when access to the field is limited or impossible, for example, due to travel restrictions posed by a civil war or a pandemic. I also explain how to make a call on the data that is grounded in and utilizes QCA based on prior emails and surveys, which can be helpful when triangulating results after returning from the field.

The type of QCA highlighted in this book is csQCA, which is the simplest form of QCA. However, with proper strategies and methods in place, it can be used for complex analyses. I argue that csQCA is better for analysis based on a relational and dynamic understanding of social phenomena that can be explained through mechanisms, strategies, and processes. This method further clarifies these complex social phenomena by classifying them as either active (1) or inactive (0), rather than assigning a numerical value to indicate strength. The limitations of csQCA are also assessed, as many QCA users focus instead on fsQCA. The need to render the complex phenomena into Boolean logic (1 or 0) could be seen as a limitation in some circumstances. The recommendation for addressing the key limitations of QCA is consistent and thorough triangulation of the results that integrates descriptive ethnographic data and additional contextual analyses, as there are issues and causalities that cannot be adequately conveyed by mere QCA tables. This systematic augmentation is fully unpacked in Chapter 4 through an in-depth, process-tracing analysis of how particular causal conditions relate to different outcomes.

Based on my literature review of QCA, this book provides three major contributions that are lacking in or absent from the existing publications on QCA, or need further elaboration:

1 There is no comparable hands-on guide for how to apply the method and what needs to be considered in practice when writing analyses about causal relations drawn from the collected data.
2 The methods of QCA are often reliant on statistical programs and software. However, the methods described in this book will be actionable even for those who do not use these tools.
3 This is not a complex, abstract, or long methodological guidebook; rather, it is a new type of short, practice-oriented book that shows how the method is applied to a database and offers a concrete analysis.

Situating the book

There is a dire need for methodological approaches that can help researchers with systematic and comparative analyses on how complex interactions influence outcomes in policy making. This book will show how, in practice, one can triangulate ethnographic and other data across many cases with different explanatory factors to provide more robust explanations of complex dynamics and make sense of the world. To do this, it is necessary to have concrete cases and not speak only abstractly. I base my insights and recommendations on over a decade of data collection, including extensive periods of ethnographic field research and systematic text-based data collection. In this method, these data sources come together to illustrate how QCA can be used to analyze a multiple data source database that includes results from multiple case studies. I will show, step by step, how I made methodological choices in my research, with a focus on explaining the outcomes of investment politics and movement actions in the political economy and ecology of mining and resources in Brazil and India. While this book is focused on utilizing the csQCA method, readers interested in these empirical issues will also find this book valuable.

A strong point of this book is that it shows, in practice, how an analytical and conceptual framework can be easily adapted to other complex scenarios, for example, different types of resistance strategies, political games, and the study of varying political and economic outcomes. Even though this framework is complex and yields a rich analysis, the sections are presented in this analysis in a way that makes it accessible and actionable. Researchers who are interested in expanding their methodological toolkit to include QCA will find this book particularly useful. This method appeals across many disciplines, as it can be applied to a myriad of research questions, especially in comparative politics, political economy, development, political ecology, economics, and social movement studies. The book can be used as a guide for methodology courses tackling the integration of systematic comparative approaches, which need publications that illustrate how QCA and other comparative analyses can be applied in practice. Other courses that are not strictly methodological can also use this book, as it offers detailed explanations of important dynamics in the global political economy, globalization, and environmental justice struggles. This book offers insight into what strategies have worked to solve pressing sustainability problems in different places and how to choose which interactions and issues should be considered with a thorough analysis. The main contribution of this book is to offer ways to assess complex causalities—for example, what are the necessary and sufficient conditions for achieving social movement goals—that go beyond simple characterizations of conflict types or causalities. Following the advice of QCA methodology (Ragin 2014), I will demonstrate with carefully curated examples how to corroborate claims of sufficiency of causal patterns with evidence coming from empirical cases, which are observed via field research and other data collection methods.

I hope this book will motivate researchers and students to use QCA as an effective method to compare cases and possible relations, causalities, and dynamics, beyond simply identifying and measuring outcomes. I offer a hands-on, practical guide to using QCA to systematically explain the influence of social movements and other resistance actors on different political and economic outcomes. It is necessary to pick a real-world set of cases to truly appreciate and show the applicability of QCA, and I argue that several case studies need to be studied thoroughly, via field research, for QCA results to be robust and for the method to come to fruition. Moreover, a real-world hypothesis and research-question-based theoretical framework is needed to align the QCA application to particular theoretical traditions, within which it then offers more grounded answers on complex interactions and outcomes. I will work through the following key question: How can one rigorously and systematically study the causalities, dynamics, and outcomes of social movement actions? This book offers a methodological and theoretically robust guide to delve into this empirical question. Practical examples demonstrate how to analyze the multiple outcomes of social movements, nongovernmental organizations (NGOs), and armed resistance actors systematically, across multiple contingencies and contexts, and to tease out the role of different causal condition complexes. The in-depth analysis of Indian and Brazilian social movement dynamics is used as a concrete example of the method in practice. These examples were picked for the book because the temporal and geographic differences in the cases show the wide applicability of the methodology.

Note

1 Hume was an early philosopher foregrounding the theory, epistemology, and methodology of causal inferences and induction based on empirical observations. He discussed the logic of necessary causalities, and causal conjunctions, in detail. Hume's take on causation comes close to the probabilistic take on QCA—which I focus on in this book—in that he questions whether there are naturally fixed or deterministic cause-effect relations, arguing rather that these are rooted to a great extent in the observers' perceptions. Thus, one needs to be aware of one's own custom of understanding the world when making causal claims. However, Hume does not eschew the use of causal analysis, but he makes important notes on the epistemology behind such reasoning. This same kind of approach is visible also in QCAs Boolean logic and especially its probabilistic take (see Hitchcock 2018). For more on Hume, please see, for example, De Pierris and Friedman (2018). Popper's notes on theory falsification and his critique of universal claims based on induction can be well-addressed and taken into account by QCA. For example, if one claims—based on seeing only white swans thus far—that all swans are white, one makes an impossible universal claim because this kind of induction cannot prove that this would be so. When the first black swan is noted, one becomes aware of the danger of such inductions. QCA has used this premise by Popper to show how one should instead focus on robust sufficiency when making causal analyses and claims (Dușa 2019).

1 Systematic data collection and analysis

Multi-sited political ethnography, QCA, and other methods for assessing complex causalities

Chapter Abstract: *This chapter explains what Qualitative Comparative Analysis (QCA) is and how it can be used and combined with other methodological approaches. The chapter also explains how I conducted the field research that provides the illustrative data for this book. This transparent guide to the fieldwork approach aids in demonstrating how QCA can be utilized from the first moment of fieldwork through to the final data analysis. This will be particularly helpful for those struggling with the selection of proper methods, when to use QCA, and how to justify the use of QCA. Detailed tables, which uncover the protocols through which the causal conditions and factors are identified as being active or not, are offered as guidelines on how these tables should be crafted to make the analysis transparent and replicable. In this chapter, there is a discussion of when to use QCA in its different variations (e.g., crisp-set, fuzzy-logic, multi-value, temporal) and how to identify when it is not a suitable method. The limitations of this approach are explored, and insight is offered on how these limitations can and should be addressed.*

QCA guidebooks, tools, and aims

Traditionally, QCA has been primarily seen as the best tool for case-oriented studies that have a moderate number of cases, what is called a medium-*n* study. However, the uses of QCA have expanded, through the introduction of new techniques, to include studies with more cases (larger *n*) used alongside studies with fewer, more detailed cases (small *n*) (Rihoux 2020). The use of QCA has even expanded beyond academia to policy-making circles, where it can be used to perform meta-analyses of projects, policies, and other cases observed in real-life settings (Rihoux 2016). This book will use a medium-*n* example to show how to use QCA across a database with 23 total cases in order to assess the possible causal linkages between 22 causal conditions and several political and economic outcomes. It should be noted that these causal conditions can also be called explanatory factors, and they can also include strategies.

I recommend reading this book in parallel with a more general QCA guidebook. The most recent (and excellent) guide on how to design and apply QCA studies is Mello's (2021) *Qualitative Comparative Analysis: Research Design and Application*. Kahwati and Kane's (2019) *Qualitative Comparative Analysis in Mixed Methods Research and Evaluation* focuses on helping students to apply QCA in mixed-methods research designs and contributes to mixed-methods textbooks. A useful complement to this mixed-methods textbook is the chapter by Rihoux, Concha, and Lobe (2021), which addresses more specifically how to utilize multiple case studies. These discussions are linked with the broader methodologies of process tracing, which aim to uncover causal mechanisms and the kind of empirical evidence that could be used to look for them, and also linked with how to sequence QCA with process tracing (Beach and Pedersen 2019; Schneider and Rohlfing 2013). The discussions here are part of this broader analysis of processes and causal mechanisms: In particular, in this project I was interested in identifying and following the key causal mechanisms and paths that might explain how resistance might impact global natural resource flows. My ethnographic approach was based on process tracing in the sense of not focusing on the broadest possible set of things to observe (as in traditional ethnography in a single place), but instead tracing the process of the global commodity boom of 2005–2015 and observing when and how this was possibly resisted. This constituted a multi-site, process-tracing exercise on two key processes: The pushing and resisting processes. Later, I divided this focus into more specific mechanisms, such as resistance strategies, observing the processes through which these, and especially their combinations, might have been causally linked to different kinds of outcomes. I found QCA to be an excellent tool to utilize for this fine-grained process tracing, which takes place later on in this book.

Like other broad guidebooks that deal with QCA, the previously mentioned books primarily focus on introducing the methodology and explaining it step-by-step. Other useful books of this nature include *Configurational Comparative Methods: Qualitative Comparative Analysis (QCA) and Related Techniques*, edited by the pioneers of QCA methodology, Rihoux and Ragin (2009). These contributions all are substantially different from my book and the work on which it is based. To really master the QCA method, I recommend reading these more abstract, introductory books, which contain some examples of application, in addition to this book, which focuses on how the method is applied in practice. One should also always stay informed about the latest summarizing review articles and book chapters on the subject. For example, Rihoux (2020) provides an updated review of the state-of-the-art in QCA research, while Thomann and Maggetti (2020) offer valuable advice on how to design QCA-based studies.

The QCA method has also been criticized from a quantitative methods perspective, as well as from other viewpoints [see the Symposium in *Sociological Methodology* 44(1)), with contributions from Ragin, Collier, and many others]. Vaisey (2014) and Ragin (2014), among others, provide good answers to these critiques, showing their many weaknesses and misunderstandings. Most of these critiques are based on assumptions that approach QCA from the logic of conventional quantitative methods. A typical misunderstanding of QCA is related to it being a configurational method, not a method to study interactions between all factors. QCA solution terms refer not to interactions but to configurations (which is the concept that should be used): This refers to "the result of additive processes reaching a threshold" (Vaisey 2014). Most of the critiques against QCA have also been leveled against other methods that usually focus on finding parsimonious solutions or providing overtly complex algorithmic tools (Collier 2014).[1] Simplicity and intuitive reasoning are recommended across techniques, rather than using very complex and complicated methods or computational tools if there is no apparent or clear need. These methods and tools should only be introduced later after careful consideration of whether they are truly needed. This decision should also include a consideration of how much extra time and effort would be needed to master and utilize more complex methods and tools and what would be gained from their implementation. David Collier (2014) recommends that QCA users abandon complex algorithm tools and simplify the method. I follow his advice here; I do not make much use of the typical, complex QCA algorithm tools but instead base my analysis on very rich and detailed, intimate case knowledge. Ragin (2014) also recommends this approach as a better solution than the use of invented counterfactuals, if one has knowledge available on the studied cases. Besides my book, the importance of deep knowledge of cases, understood as complex and dynamic wholes, and their comparison via QCA are also presented by Gerrits and Verweij (2018). Their book, *The Evaluation of Complex Infrastructure Projects: A Guide to Qualitative Comparative Analysis*, contains an empirical and methodological approach that is akin and complementary to the focus on investment politics herein.

Normally QCA explores the role of approximately three to seven conditions, due to the issue of increasing limited diversity. The problem of limited diversity refers to a set-theoretic approach, wherein one does not want to have too many logical remainders, that is, causal condition complexes that are not covered by the QCA combinations, which are the cases with a specific set of explanatory and outcome factors (Rihoux and De Meur 2009). To accommodate this, I divided the 22 explanatory factors into different sets and observed the same outcomes for these different sets. These are both important steps, because in the typical progression of QCA one needs to first consider a larger array of explanatory factors and then focus on those factors that are found to be the most important. Marx and Duşa (2011) provide helpful advice and benchmarks for considering the number of case conditions to use in different QCA applications. The contribution here is to show how one set of conditions, focusing on movement strategies, can be juxtaposed with another set of conditions, which focuses on contextual and contingency factors, to see which set better explains the outcomes. I also mix between these sets of factors to look for combinations. I did this because political ethnography, and especially multi-sited ethnography, produces a myriad of different possible explanations and factors pertinent to those explanations that could matter in different cases. When one adopts QCA based on this type of field research, guidance is needed on how to apply the method when one needs to take complexity seriously to be able to draw meaningful conclusions. One cannot just see the world and attempt to explain it accurately via limited and very broad factors.

Normally QCA is not applied to ethnographically oriented data. Ethnographically oriented research tries to produce thick descriptions and understanding of complexities instead of parsimonious explanations on more generalizable mechanisms, which is more akin to typical QCA. However, I argue that QCA-type approaches can be used for making sense of complex, multi-sited, political ethnographic data. However, the key focus is not on trying to produce just the most parsimonious solution, but instead offering a tool for systematic data handling, comparisons, and drawing probabilistic findings from complex data sets. Thus, this book partakes in broadening the uses of QCA, which follows the trend in the field, specifically in the expansion of the use of more probabilistic procedures (Rihoux 2016).

Parsimonious explanations can also be pursued, but I will show how this is not the only way QCA should be applied. I provide a contribution to the bulk of QCA usages, especially by showing how medium-n databases across an abnormally large number of causal conditions (over 20) and outcomes (over 5) can be made sense of via an approach that is primarily and initially probabilistic, yet is in sequence parsimony-seeking.

The prior usages of QCA have based their logic mostly on set-theoretical and particular logical inferences, for example, through the usage of Boolean logic. This discussion opens up the prospect that one should take into consideration even logically possible combinations that are not present in the actual data sets, what are called logical remainders (Rihoux and De Meur 2009). These logical remainders are useful for making further analyses, but QCA users normally try to avoid having too many of them by limiting the number of conditions, as having too many conditions leads to many individualized case explanations. However, I will show, through multi-sited ethnography data that are reported via QCA tables, that one cannot and should not try to steer reality too much toward more parsimonious explanations that go beyond the nuance of the actual reality. Instead, one should use the tool in these kinds of data sets and situations for systematic comparison in order to identify the possible generalizable dynamics. There are necessary and sufficient causal condition complexes and factors that can be uncovered through a real-world database across 22 conditions and 23 cases. I would also like to note that the utilization of invented case scenarios is not recommended or necessary in analysis that is based on a limited data set of observed, real-world scenarios that are already sufficiently complex. However, I will show how the guidance in existing QCA technical guidebooks (e.g., in Rihoux and De Meur 2009, see box 3.6) on how to resolve contradictory configurations and rework the conditions and their sets is helpful and can be used in practice.

Specific technical tools can be used and are recommended when conducting QCA, especially across a database as vast as the one I used in my research. I used the Excel QCA add-in developed by Lasse Cronqvist (2019) to check my results and each subtable, which I obtained by first manually analyzing the tables and going through each combination. I highly recommend this Excel tool, which is free, open-access, and easy to use. It provides help with double-checking the truth table findings and determining the implicants (the cases and their factors that produced the outcome studied) and solutions (the different truth formulas). In addition, the tool is useful as it allows for checking what the analysis would be in cases where logical remainders are included. It also allows for quickly checking what would explain the 0 outcomes. When I refer to the "Excel tool" in this book, I refer to this QCA tool.

Thiem and Duşa (2013) discuss the issue of whether to use parsimonious or intermediate solution terms in QCA, which currently divides opinion. I show how one can pursue both and how even individualized accounts do serve a purpose. Most importantly, I put much more value on a probabilistic approach, wherein I observe, for example, that a set of conditions was present in most of the cases. There are so many contextual and contingency differences in the real world—especially when comparing across different cases in different parts of the Brazilian and Indian realities—that one cannot assume a parsimonious explanation can be found. Instead, I show how particular sets of conditions explain a particular set of cases, depending on the context, for example, civil war or peaceful setting. The Excel tool is helpful as it can be used to quickly go through different sets of case combinations and condition sets, selecting these based on contextual and other limitations that surface.

There are other tools that can be used in QCA and publications that offer guidance for their usage. For example, Thiem and Duşa (2013) focus on offering advice on how to use QCA with the R software package for statistical computing. They discuss how to use crisp-set, multi-value, and fuzzy-logic versions of QCA in R software, with the assumption that the reader already knows the fundamentals of QCA and R. In comparison, this book will offer guidance and demonstrate how one can perform good QCA without needing to learn software that is typically too complex or complicated for noninstructed users. This type of approach to QCA has been called for even by those who take a more critical stance toward the method: For example, Collier (2014), does not favor adopting the new algorithms and programs designed to study QCA tables, but instead prefers to refocus attention on case-based research, process tracing, and other conventional qualitative methods, which should be the primary method. This book answers the call for simpler approaches that show how QCA can be used. I demonstrate how necessary and sufficient causal condition complexes can be identified through Excel-based tables that are divided into subsets of truth tables that are easily read and interpreted. These tables are opened up and analyzed in this book, showing how they can be unpacked in practice.

On one hand, the added value of multi-sited ethnography here is to provide a broader comparison than is typical and not a detailed case study, which already abound in the resistance and mining literature. On the other hand, the usage of csQCA, and the several case studies that are compared, signifies that more abstraction and generalization are required to allow for conceptualization that captures the heterogeneity across the cases and also allows for a comparison of recurring dynamics across the contexts.

Writing a methodology section on multi-sited ethnography and QCA

Each research project should produce a description of the methodology used and justifications for the choices made. What follows is a concrete example of how that methodology section should be written, based partially on the methodological annex of *Iron Will: Global Extractivism and Mining Resistance in Brazil and India* (Kröger 2020). I wrote *Iron Will* using a subset of the empirical materials that I use in this book to support my examples. While this book focuses on how to the use the method, the focus in *Iron Will* is the analysis resulting from use of the method. The text that follows can be used as an example of how to justify the methodological choices of QCA and multi-sited political ethnography.

The data that make up the concrete examples used in this book were collected utilizing multi-sited ethnography (Marcus 1995) primarily conducted in 2010–2016. My multi-sited ethnographic approach has a particular focus on political ethnography (Schatz 2009). Due to the immersive nature of political ethnography and my long-term engagement in the field, I was able to gather a rich bank of empirical materials, which allowed me to draw comparisons that I used in the analyses of process and power in my research locations. The knowledge creation in this method was accomplished in part by an engaged, detail-oriented, and long-term exposure to the lives and lived experiences of the informants in the case study locations (see Auyero and Swistun 2009). In addition to participant observation, this method also incorporated semistructured interviews. The method has many applications and has been used to study routine politics (for example, established political practices such as elections), violent settings, civil war, and the social and environmental dilemmas that arise in the face of investment projects (Auyero 2007; Auyero and Swistun 2009; Schatz 2009). The ethnographic approach I chose could be called a world-political ethnography, which falls closest to the approach that is discussed by MacKay and Levin (2015). Multi-sited ethnography is not designed to be limited or focused on a particular "culture," place, or ethnic group; rather, it uses ethnographic approaches to study global processes. This approach is then combined with political ethnography, an approach to ethnography with the goal of making ethnographic data useful for political analysis through a focus on power relations. The combination of these two approaches resulted in this world-political ethnographic approach, which in this case was focused on investment politics.

My empirical material consisted of a very large database filled with the hundreds of interviews and extensive field notes that I collected while in the countries at my respective research sites. In addition to being large, the entries in the database are very detailed on account of the rich materials that I used to construct them. To find informants and collect interviews, I used the snowball method, as this helped me to access research informants that otherwise might have been difficult to identify. In addition to this on-the-ground research, I also conducted an extensive literature review and made a detailed overview of other secondary documents. From this material, I extracted a more limited data set using csQCA to provide a systematic and more condensed explanation than only ethnography for such a broad study area can provide. QCA is a set-theoretic method that helped in identifying detailed, causal condition complexes and their possible causal relations with differing outcomes (Ragin 1987; Rihoux 2008; Small 2013). QCA is a technique that makes possible and even facilitates the analysis of multiple causation and interaction effects, wherein a specific outcome could be reached via different causal "paths" (Rihoux 2008, 726). Moreover, the QCA method is useful to summarize data, develop theories, produce new hypotheses, and detect logical contradictions (Brown and Boswell 1995, 1511). In the new land rush literature, these are all pressing demands (Edelman, Oya, and Borras 2013).

I identified several causal factors and observed whether their presence or absence could help explain the outcomes. For the analysis, I assigned these causal factors different letters and numbers (see Table 3.3). The obvious constraint in csQCA is the Boolean logic, which is used to mark a causal condition as either active (1) or inactive (0) in a given case. This initial determination was supplemented by my depiction and analysis of political ethnographic observation and interviews. This methodological triangulation, through the inclusion of ethnography in causal analysis, answers the call by Small (2013) to strengthen the understanding among both ethnographers and quantitative researchers of the potential of ethnographic data in conducting causal analysis—a topic that has not received sufficient attention.

The QCA truth tables, which summarize the causal paths leading to particular outcomes, are tools that can quickly convey the main differences to a reader. The decision between a 1 and a 0 is always an arbitrary choice, even though modern computers work by Boolean logic and manage to perform very complex analyses. One can use QCA in the same way, running multiple rounds of analysis, going back and forth between the data, observations, and analysis, further specifying the key causal conditions, adding new conditions, refining and specifying old conditions, and removing some. In the end, one can arrive at multiple paths that have both necessary and sufficient causal conditions and varying outcomes.

My application of QCA first included all factors identified during the field research and literature review as potential causal conditions. These causal conditions covered not only resistance but also contexts, contingencies, corporate, government, third party, and other conditions. They were next delimited and refined into key pathways through repeated rounds of QCA. This approach contributes to overcoming the dilemma of causal attribution that Bosi and Giugni (2012) view as the key challenge in outcome scholarship. One motivation for this was the demand in existing studies, such as by Suh (2012, 98) who argues, "A more sophisticated research design and an innovative methodological approach are needed to reveal the causality between social movements and social changes."

An application of csQCA based on the *Dynamics of Contention* by McAdam, Tarrow, and Tilly (2001) relies on the logic of specifying and then further specifying each of the strategies, mechanisms, and dynamics. The key benefits of a well-done csQCA include its focus on uncovering multiple joint causal chains (instead of providing a far too simplistic analysis on, e.g., "resistance" or "absence of resistance"), offering transparency on how the dichotomization was performed, and the possibility of returning back to the cases, which are retained in their complexity instead of becoming blurred (as happens in variable-based regression analysis) (Giugni and Yamasaki 2009; Wagemann 2014). These aspects of the csQCA research design make it possible to understand in greater depth the importance of the quality of certain strategies versus others. An alternative approach would have examined statistical correlations or used, for example, fsQCA with intervals between 0.1 and 0.9, showing that the strategy was used less (0.1) or more (0.9) in the particular case—but such a fuzzy-set logic would require establishing 12 interval rules for quite general strategies (these ranging from 0 to 1, at 0.1 intervals). This would be a problem especially if based not on qualitative assessments but on a simplification of statistical data. Furthermore, and importantly, McAdam et al. (2010) have found some takes on fsQCA to be incompatible with a relational or dynamics of contention approach to the study of contentious politics.

Explaining the opposition to pipeline projects, McAdam et al. (2010, 424, italics in original) have argued that fsQCA would be "incompatible with calls by scholars of contention . . . for more attention to the dynamic *mechanisms* that actually account for the causal force of static variables." This may be so, if the data are mostly statistical or numerical and have not been collected right from the start based on an ingrained understanding of the world as being created through relations and mechanisms (and thus looking at the activeness or inactiveness of such mechanisms as the basic analytical categories), and if there are too many intervals in the fsQCA that is applied. However, csQCA and also fsQCA, where the value set is based on qualitative assessments having, for example, just four values,[2] are good and useful tools for exploring investment politics and social movements from the dynamics of contention perspective. Therefore with this book, I recommend that scholars of social movements and other complex, mechanisms-based explanations of the world should not steer away from the possibility of using QCA based on the critical remarks generated by the study of McAdam et al. (2010) on fsQCA, but instead refocus their attention on csQCA in these research designs (or use simple forms of fsQCA based on qualitative assessments). This call is in line with the demand for detailed, case-oriented applications of QCA, wherein dichotomization has been argued to be more favorable than gradualist perspectives (De Meur, Rihoux, and Yamasaki 2009). One cannot generalize that the usage of QCA in a particular research design would validate or invalidate the whole range of QCA techniques and approaches and thus favor or make necessary the use of other methods.

In order to use regression analysis to look for statistical correlations between outcomes and variables, I would have needed quantitative data—and this analysis would not yield support for claims on relational mechanisms. Because strategies are better understood as either used or not used in particular case areas at a particular moment, csQCA is one of the few methods that provides support for causal analysis. After a period under observation, the strategy set can change to something new. Thus, a very long, temporal, quantitative analysis of the same variable would not be possible, but the use of QCA that breaks the analysis of specific time periods into distinct tables takes into account the fact that causal conditions change. In my tables, if not otherwise indicated, the time period is 2005–2015, with resistance occurring at some period within this time.

QCA has been criticized due to "Galton's problem," in which cases that happen before or after each other are not comparable because some of them have affected the subsequent cases across time or through space, through cross-case interdependencies (Ragin and Strand 2008). I took this criticism into account and used other comparative methodologies to examine such potential impacts to clear such discrepancies from the data. I used the comparative strategy of synchronic, incorporated comparison suggested by McMichael (1992), which made it possible to track down cross-place temporal causalities, if any existed. For example, the prior successful resistance in Kudremukh and Bellary influenced the investment politics elsewhere in India, but as I tracked down these influences and conducted research on the sites that were influenced by the impact of local resistance, I could identify its role despite Galton's problem (where two or more synchronous cases might influence or "contaminate" each other). I have discussed the results of these incorporated comparisons in detail in other publications and focus here more on the process of the QCA.

QCA typically tries to find a minimal formula, an explanation that is as parsimonious as possible. I have not opted to go all the way down the road to parsimony in this sample data set, as my goal is not so much to find a generalizable outcome but rather to explain the richness of different cases where policies are made regarding investments. This allows for one to give justice to the ethnographic and case data details, without losing the particularities of each case to the overgeneralization of conditions. Thus, I recognize, for example, when only one case differed from the overall set of configurations. This adds a probabilistic dimension to the analysis. This approach also allows for not going down the road to making too broad or too dangerously simplified generalizations through the minimal formula function. Instead, I am interested in exploring how different resistance strategies, when used alone and together, might impact investment politics and showing how thinking through a QCA-type comparison can help in this task.

One must be certain to carefully justify one's methodological choices, as I demonstrated in the preceding text. In the next section, I will delve deeper into how to discuss and justify the selection of cases.

Introducing the empirical and theoretical cases

The analysis of social movements and the outcomes of their actions is a growing research field, which requires more in-depth applications of systematic and rigorous comparative analyses to provide more robust answers. This study presents in condensed form the findings of a large research project that analyzed all the major iron ore mining projects in Brazil and India between 2005 and 2015 and the potential impact that resistance and other factors had on the outcomes of these projects. I focus on providing a methodological example of how to apply and collect the required data for a systematic analysis on how social movements and other resistance actors, such as NGOs, do and do not influence political and economic outcomes, and I show how to present the findings in a snapshot way. I illustrate how a project's research design can take into consideration competing and complementary factors across a large array of potential causal conditions and contingencies that potentially explain a series of outcomes within a particular research field. This research design can be applied across a large variety of settings, and I demonstrate how it can yield valuable answers to pending questions that require systematic and comparative analyses to be uncovered instead of single case studies or analyses that have unobserved cases.

The research project whose findings are presented here was designed as a QCA from the start. The data were collected through multi-sited political ethnography across all the major iron ore mining sites of two crucial countries in the sector under consideration (iron ore and steel production). One must consider one's research design carefully in QCA as there should be no cases left unobserved. This design has been called for in reviews of how QCA has been and should be applied in social movement studies (Wagemann 2014). One should ensure that all cases across a bounded sector are analyzed, including those without the presence of resistance. The resulting database will be rich and will yield a large variety across outcomes. In the case of my data, this manifested as continued and discontinued mining operations.

A good QCA project starts with a good research base, which considers possible future caveats and objections to the research design. From the start of the research process and design of the database, it is important to focus on a particular topic as this allows one to be able to say something about a specific topic. A more focused inquiry allows for a more focused database design, which more easily supports and backs up any generalizations made. This is preferable to making claims that are too broad and are not empirically backed or theoretically bounded. It was important to focus on one sector (mining) and its subsector (iron ore) to rule out the possible impact of (sub-)sectorial dynamics. Many existing studies on social movement outcomes are too broad and general to be able to rule out the role of such dynamics, focusing, for example, on "environmental movements," which might include all kinds of tangential issues (Giugni 2004). Furthermore, the number of polities included is typically far too high to be able to isolate the role of political systems and contexts and compare their effects. QCA is an approach that prior social movement studies have found helpful in answering pending questions and in corroborating and challenging results obtained through other approaches (Giugni and Yamasaki 2009).

Bounding and identifying cases

QCA works based on a comparison of cases. It is important to open up and discuss what cases have been included in one's study. Quite often the protocol of how one has come up with the specific cases is left unmentioned, including how they were bounded and identified. Next, I will explain how I defined the cases, and this description can be helpful as an example of a methodological opening for the more detailed, method-oriented parts of a publication.

I started by mapping out the topic of my study. In this case, I focused on all the major iron ore mining areas in Brazil and India, including both existing and planned mines. In addition, I tried to understand where the export routes and ports were located. I identified the location of the most important steel mills that used the iron ore. There was no ready-made or easily accessible information on this topic. Based on this mapping, I then separated distinct cases of iron ore politics using the locality where they were taking place. Normally, these separate cases were bound by particular resistance movements or dynamics creating the differences, and the areas also were geographically distinct from each other.

The key parameter I used in bounding these cases was that each case needed to conform to sufficiently uniform dynamics. If I found multiple and different dynamics within a single case, then I subdivided this initial "case" into several discrete cases, which allowed me to further analyze these differing dynamics. This was illustrated by the Carajás mining area in Pará, Brazil, where the old mining site of Carajás showed a somewhat different set of resistance strategies used in comparison to the specific activism targeting the new, greenfield expansion of the S11D mining complex. If a large area had similar dynamics, then I did not disaggregate it into smaller parcels but discussed the largest possible contextually united area as a single case. For this reason, I did not separate Goa, India, into the south (where most of the mining was taking place) and the north, as the resistance was statewide with a very small interstate variation compared to the differences relativized by the larger comparative apparatus.

I used a methodological approach similar to that described previously for selecting and studying the conditions. That is, I added a new resistance strategy or other kind of explanatory factor when I saw one needed to be added to be able to adequately explain the case dynamics. After adding the strategy or other kind of causal condition, I then inspected the other cases to evaluate whether they also had values for that causality.

Transparency in reporting data gathering and analysis methods

Tables are helpful to illustrate for others, in a condensed way, how one has observed and understood a condition or case to be either active and present or not, that is, what observation protocols one has used. Table 1.1 explains in more detail what I studied in disaggregating investment politics. This table illustrates the mechanisms and strategies that create the resistance and the protocol through which these causal conditions were observed to be active or not in a case. In producing this table, I followed parts of the disaggregation table in Falleti and Lynch (2008, 335). Three top-level-process types influence resource use style, that is, resistance, interaction within the state, and extractive agency. These upper-level processes are the results of specific relations, summarized for the top-level processes in the table.

The conceptualization of "investment politics" used here stems from my prior research, wherein I studied not only the tree plantation (forestry) or the pulp mill (factory setting) aspects of the politics of pulp investment (prior studies on this sector mostly focused on either one or the other, separately) but both forestry and mills, which together form the "pulp investment" (Kröger 2013). This investment typically has a bounded area of impact, primarily felt within a 100-km (62-mile) radius due to the logistical costs of acquiring wood from farther away. Thus, a researcher analyzing the investment impacts and conflict dynamics can approach the different investment cases by studying this perimeter of impact where the company has operations. Similarly, for this research, I first had to find out where the investment areas for the new iron ore mining projects were; this included those that sought to either expand the existing mining areas nearby or establish greenfield mining sites. As a result of this extensive fieldwork, which mapped the locations of these investment areas, I produced Maps 1.1 and 1.2. The bounded geographical areas showcase roughly the "investment

Table 1.1 Disaggregation of processes into mechanisms and strategies in extractive politics: activeness observation protocols

Top-level process (what explains the pace and style of extractivism)	Extractive agency	Interactive processes within the state	Resistance
Process-as-type (what relations produce the top-level processes)	Direct government influence; contentious, electoral, institutional, judicial, private, and armed revolution/secessionary politics.		
Mechanism-as-example (what mechanisms and strategies create the resistance process)	Mechanism-as-indicator (how were the sample mechanisms observed to be active in a case)		
a = Organizing and politicizing a mass social movement	(a) Existence of a mass social movement organization that enjoys widespread local support. This movement also has an alternative social, symbolic, and physical space. (Examples include MST settlements, indigenous lands, and even small mining towns whose powerholders and majority have embraced heterodox stances toward mining. Examples where this strategy was not present include resistance unfolding through small expert NGOs and cases where the locals were in favor of mining.)		
b = Campaigning with heterodox, nonmodernist, anti-mining framing	(b) Existence of long-term campaigns that are against the project at hand and have produced heterodox discourses that are against the project at hand and have produced heterodox frames in relation to the Cartesian and extractivist (modernity's) understanding of nature (in this case, the environment where the mineral is located as something that can be dominated ("developed") by humans and/or denominated as a mere "natural resource." (Examples of how the presence of this strategy was detected include the heterodox frame's replication in important media, e.g., intensive internet activism where, for example, blogs are followed by a large audience, as in Goa. Examples where this strategy was deemed not to be active include cases where mining unions led the resistance and focused on changing the style of mining, instead of being anti-mining, and cases where the resistance did not engage in marked public campaigning for various reasons, such as in a number of cases in Odisha and Chhattisgarh, India.)		
c = Physically nonviolent mass protesting that is noted	(c) The existence of protest acts targeting an extractive operation that are physical (e.g., marches, sit-ins, road blockages, land occupations), do not use physical violence against humans, and are noted in the public media by the authorities or by the target.		
d = Networking with other resistance groups			
E = Embedding the state in electoral, institutional, and/or judicial politics while retaining autonomy			
e1 = Using electoral politics via targeted voting of politicians opposing mining or allying with politicians seeking mine closure, while retaining movement autonomy			
e2 = Using institutional politics while retaining autonomy			
e3 = Using judicial politics via starting litigation in court against the project			
f = Participation in private politics initiatives of companies (CSR, etc.) where an agreement is reached			

(d) The existence of a strong resistance network consisting of many different actors; the replication of the progenitor resistance actor model by other social actors in the area or national or transnational coalition building.

(e) Autonomy: Continued, resistance-controlled internal decision-making and the utilization of external resources even after state embedding. (Ethnographic material where several actors, inside and outside particular groups, are asked whether the group has retained autonomy or whether it has been co-opted, captured, or moved toward lesser autonomy via corporate or state embedding into powerful positions in the resistance group.)

(e1) Proof of the writing of memoranda of understanding (MOUs) about resisting a project with candidates for political posts (resistance group insiders or outsiders) before elections (as in Keonjhar); the integration of politicians into the resistance front and their endorsement of the resistance viewpoints (as in the case of Casa de Pedra); or the co-organization of events directed at blocking a project by the civil society and elected decision makers (as in Mina del Rey).

(e2) Institutional embedding, for example, by acquiring progressive state-actor-led investigations via advocacy (as in the case of the Shah Commission), successfully demanding that regulatory institutions intervene to uphold the rule of law (as in the activation of the powerful but seldom successfully used state "ombudsman" office of Lokayukta in Bellary), occupying key institutions (as in the embedding of the INCRA state land institute by the MST), and/or crafting new institutions (as in the creation of the PESA, FRA, and Right to Information Acts and their respective institutions in India).

(e3) A suit against a project is filed in court by resistance organizations, or a class action suit is raised through a public prosecutor.

(f) Resistance group receives material benefits directly from companies or organizations or from state institutions over which the company has power (as in the case of Vale-MST in Pará and Maranhão); proof that the resistance works through the companies' CSR tools (stakeholder dialogues) to try to fix a deal, and an agreement is reached.

areas" whose various investment politics I analyzed. These investment politics included the push to extract more minerals and the resistance to this extraction, as manifested in the physical areas in question. This resistance manifested physically as either advancing or blocking the expansion of extraction. Thus, this was a study of the politics at the points of extraction that sought to curb the expansion of new, open-pit, iron ore mines. When mining areas exposed differing political or conflict dynamics or other key features, such as different strategy sets, I divided them into a study of distinct "investment politics" to be compared for their differences in causal conditions.

There are specific field research skills that compound as a researcher goes to different investment sites and that, over the years, result in the development of an efficient way to do field research. These skills include doing expert and other interviews, performing field visits, triangulating across the varying data sources that are available to be collected, and verifying the sayings of people by actually visiting the sites. In addition, the researcher learns how to "hang around" in the areas, and return to them, to delve deeper into the cases. These field research skills that develop when conducting comparative research on investment politics can be used in subsequent research projects, which allows for a relatively short amount of time to be spent in each area visited (at least in comparison to classical single-place ethnography). This allows a researcher to conduct a single-author, multi-sited political ethnography of broad and complex phenomena, such as global extractive investments. In my research on iron ore mining and resistance, I spent six months collecting data in India (in 2010 and 2012–2013) and six months in Brazil (in 2011 and 2014). However, the overall time spent gathering all the other information on the investment sites, including the data for the areas that I did not personally visit, took several years and was based on several years of prior research on natural resource politics in different parts of the world's rural areas, especially in South America.

Field research generally requires making many compromises when collecting data due to time and other constraints. This is also true for multi-sited ethnography as there are limits on who can be interviewed, how many interviews can be conducted overall, and what can be observed for what length of time. It is important to think through why one is making specific decisions about how to conduct one's fieldwork. In my research, I used my focus on the political ethnography of the processes that influence extractivism via resistance to help guide my choices.[3] To this end, I focused on finding informants who were intimately connected to these processes. This meant that most of these informants were movement leaders, coordinators, well-known activists, scholars, NGO directors, bureaucrats, lawyers, journalists, politicians, and other experts. These interviewees were key policy makers. I also interviewed company personnel and other pro-mining social actors. I do not mention the individuals I interviewed by name here, as the situations in India and Brazil for many of them are increasingly difficult. Revealing their names could lead to serious problems for them. In addition, some of them spoke confidentially or on the promise of anonymity.

As mentioned, fieldwork requires compromises, so while I visited many of the areas that are marked on the maps, I was not able to go to all of them.

Map 1.1 Displays the major iron ore mining project areas of India between 2005 and 2015, which I studied.[4] The bounded geographical areas on the map are different sizes, referring to the approximate extensions of the mining case area.

26 *Systematic data collection and analysis*

Map 1.2 Presents the main iron ore extraction areas of Brazil that are discussed herein.[5]

It is important to be transparent about the places where one conducts first-person field research or participant observation, and it is also important to be transparent about the places one does not visit and why. While I was in India, I managed to conduct many interviews with the organizations, resistance leaders, and other involved actors from Bellary (3) and Tiruvannamalai (5) in other places, so it was not as pressing to visit these sites directly. There were other areas in India that were embroiled in armed conflicts; thus, it was either not recommended or even forbidden to enter these areas. This was the case in West Singhbhum (8), Dantewada (11), Rowghat (12), Dalli Rajah (13), and Manpur (14) (the number after the name corresponds to the legend on Map 1.1). To compensate for not being able to directly enter these areas, I traveled close to them and invited locals to join me at those locations. Using this technique, I was able to have discussions with over 200 people from the affected areas for my database. These discussions ranged from several hours to multiple days. They were very important to help me develop a sense of the case, even though I could not personally go to these sites due to the danger. In Brazil, I also did not go to all of the locations, for example, Minas-Rio, although I found this to be problematic later on as I had to rely on existing data about the area. Later in this book, I will use this example to explore how crucial it is not to rely on data produced by others; rather, one should strive to conduct ethnographic observation across all the cases personally (other researchers can also join the endeavor, at the same time or other times in the same area). This is important because the observations depend quite a bit on the theoretical and onto-epistemological worldview and experience of each observer. One also cannot have complete certainty about the quality of data that others have produced.

In some cases, the reason I did not visit the areas personally was because there were already extensive research and publications on these areas. This was a partial caveat and turned out to be a problem in the end, as one does get a better picture if all the cases have been personally observed. However, in the real world, time can be a constraint. In addition, there should be space for ambitious research projects that cover many cases, and thus, secondary data may be necessary to some extent. However, for QCA, where each single case matters equally, this is a problem that needs to be addressed. Thus, I show how to discuss the weaknesses and possible discrepancies in data in the cases not observed directly by the researcher. For example, some of the notes on mining projects written in the Environmental Justice Organizations, Liabilities and Trade (EJOLT) Atlas (ejatlas.org) were used to triangulate and supplement the findings. I later had to recalibrate these cases based on new information from people who knew the cases better.

To be able to conduct multi-sited ethnography, or to do QCA in general, the context and polities studied, with their cultural and other particularities, should first be well-understood. One also should have in-depth experience from at least a few of the case areas. This experience needs to be clear for readers, and any gaps in or lack of experience should be reported. My studies of rural Brazil began in 2003 when I did my master's thesis on the interactions between a resistance movement and eucalyptus plantations. While my first research on Brazil centered on tree plantations, I have been interested in the mining areas for many years as well. The mining areas have been my principal research focus since 2010. This facet of my research interest started with a participant observation in Carajás, which includes mining areas. I was able to delve more deeply into the mining dynamics in 2011 during a period of participant observation in the Palmares settlements of the MST in Parauebebas municipality. In this same time frame, I also spent time inside and around the Carajás mine next to Palmares. I thought it was particularly compelling to trace the commodity chain of the iron ore, and I looked into pig iron and charcoal production. I also became more interested in the study of the broader mining politics. There were particularly compelling transportation politics around the export railroad line in Marabá and Western Maranhão. However, I did not study all possible cases in such great detail, for example, the cases of Minas Gerais, Bahia, or Mato Grosso do Sul. It should be noted that there are many iron ore mines and related conflicts in Minas Gerais, but this is an area that has already been covered quite extensively by other researchers. Additionally, there is such breadth and depth to this topic that it deserves full treatment and a systematic analysis and explanation in a separate study. For both of these reasons, I chose not to go to the area myself. Another reason was that my database was already very large and becoming hard to handle. The more cases one studies in detail, the more complex things can get. This is a key reason why QCA should be utilized at each stage when adding a new case and why research project design is important.

Existing databases on the same cases can be used to triangulate one's results in a way that verifies whether one's own observations are accurate. I identified several such databases in Brazil that I used for triangulation. The "Map of Environmental Conflicts in Minas Gerais" includes iron ore conflicts. This map is produced by the Grupo de Estudos em Temáticas Ambientais from the Federal University of Minas Gerais, which is a study group on environmental themes.[6] I found another similar, data-rich mapping project that included some of the relevant iron ore conflicts from The Oswaldo Cruz Foundation (Fiocruz). Both of these resources proved to be appropriate and helpful to triangulate my findings.

Those cases not relevant for the key research question or hypothesis can be left out after justification. My focus was on explaining new iron ore expansion, in either established mines or new ventures, that had created new political dynamics worthy of investigation. This meant that some operations were left out, as there were no new or meaningful data to be had from them to support exploration of the key question and hypothesis. These cases were, however, tangentially present, although not included directly in the QCA tables. Brazil had the world's four largest iron ore mines: (1) Carajás [7.27 billion tons (bt) of reserves and a production of 106.7 million tons (mt) in 2012, Vale]; (2) Samarco Alegria [2.97 bt of reserves, 21.8 mt of production, owned by Vale (50%) and BHB (50%)];[7] (3) Minas Itabiritos (2.78 bt, 31.8 mt, Vale); and (4) Vargem Grande (2.53 bt, 22.6 mt, Vale).[8] The last three in this list are in Minas Gerais. In these older mining operations, even when there was expansion, it was usually happening inside the existing mines and did not produce notable conflicts. Thus, I did not study the politics around these sites in detail, although these cases also produced grievances even before the tailings dam disasters of mid-2010s,[9] because my interest lay in an examination of the varied resistance politics in Minas Gerais. I found several projects that were particularly interesting because the mines were developed on land that had not already been mined. I found that in these cases, there tended to be greater problems and resistance efforts. It is worth mentioning that in some cases a new plan to reopen an old mine by Vale stirred up problems. Yet, in other cases, even those with allegations of atrocities, there were no mass social movements. For example, in 2015 there was no mass uprising in Itabira (where the Vale company was founded and the Minas Itabiritos has been since the 1940s), despite claims by the anti-Vale network that Vale was responsible for putting people in slave-labor-like conditions.[10]

In some of the cases, it was difficult to find many people acquainted well enough with the mining politics in the area to be considered as potential informants. A small number of informants is a risk for data integrity. This happened during the discussions I had in Keonjhar, which is located in Odisha, India. In this area, I was visiting mining regions and areas where the mining projects had stalled. While I was in these regions, I was able to learn about specific and nuanced dynamics and issues that were quite salient in those remote rural villages but that had received little or no public coverage in the capital. However, just because the people in the capital were not aware of these particular issues, did not mean they were unimportant. Thus, in a case like this—while I had to rely on a small number of informants—it was important to include the information in my analysis.

Other compromises that I had to make were related to language. I can comfortably speak Portuguese, Spanish, and English, so in Brazil there was no need to have a translator present for the interviews. This allowed me to interview anyone I encountered without needing to make further logistical arrangements. However, in India translation was required as I do not speak Hindi or the other local Indian languages. This limitation proved to be particularly challenging when meeting the Adivasi indigenous peoples. I utilized the help of translators to converse with non-English speakers, yet this led to some issues logistically as translators were hard to find for localized Adivasi languages. In addition, the translators often had their own ideas about the topics of the interviews. These ideas seemed to become intermeshed with translations to the degree that I could not always decipher the thoughts that belonged to my interviewee and those that had come from the translator. This was especially problematic and even seemed to have an effect on the quality of the data. My methodological apparatus at times required that I make an extended explanation of what I meant by strategies and other key concepts. I then wanted my informants to reflect upon these concepts and how they manifested in their respective cases. It was difficult to always know definitively whether the translator had been accurate in conveying my explanation and also whether the response represented only the ideas of my informant. As a result, I mostly avoided directly quoting the data from these translated interviews. I also limited the number of translated interviews as much as possible (these represented only a small fraction of the overall interview database), and I focused instead on the English-speaking Indian informants. At other times, I talked to several Adivasis together, so that those who spoke English could check with each other and convey their meanings to me.

To aid in my data analysis, I had some of the recorded interviews transcribed. This transcription resulted in a 50,000-word document, which I used during my analysis to check for anything I had missed in my handwritten field memos. While my field memos covered most key points, having the transcribed backup was useful for checking and verifying the quotations. I lost over half of my transcription interview data when the iPod Touch I used for recording the interviews crashed and the data could not be retrieved as it had been overridden. I recommend using interview tools that allow for external backing up of the data, even those that can be regularly uploaded to cloud storage. This was not yet a feasible option in 2010–2013 in the remote areas of India and Brazil. However, I did have extensive handwritten interview and field research memos as a backup, and I also checked the quotes from the informants after returning from the field.

It is highly recommended to verify or triangulate the data that are collected in a multi-sited ethnography. There are many different methods and approaches to this triangulation, and the ways in which one accomplishes one's triangulation should be explicitly explained. I used multiple forms of verification for my research material, as different methods, data, theories, and scholarly discussions addressed different facets of my overarching research goals. I will now run through a few of the main methods of triangulation that I used in my project. The data can be corroborated through data triangulation; in my project this included reading existing academic publications, media accounts, and other secondary documents. In addition, I talked to other scholars and experts at conferences and elsewhere. I also had to triangulate the methods that I employed in my research. This included using other types of methods to verify the accounts of my informants. For example, when an informant described a particular mine or mine expansion, I would look at satellite images to see whether there was a mine or a mine expansion in the place they had mentioned. I needed to do this to evaluate whether their accounts were precise or trustworthy, especially in areas that I did not personally observe. I also looked for available statistics and information on mining areas, volumes, and expansion plans from official, company, and other sources. While I was still in the field, I tried to physically visit the areas that were mentioned. While in these areas, I always I tried to talk to the people about the local topography and politics. Another important triangulation approach for me was researcher-analysis triangulation, which is a way to check whether the results I see in my analysis are also seen by others. I employed a two-fold approach to this aspect of the triangulation. I asked other scholars who had been doing research in the area what they had found and compared their findings to my findings. I also utilized field research assistants in some of the cases to help me with a variety of tasks. In some cases, I had them read through the transcripts from the interviews and draw their own analytical findings. Similar to how I compared other researchers' findings to my own, I took their findings and juxtaposed them with my analysis. As a final step in the triangulation of my research, I engaged in theoretical triangulation. In this triangulation, one develops complementary hypotheses and explanatory factors that approach the data from very different theoretical viewpoints. These viewpoints are used to investigate the political context, contingency, and movement strategies in order to identify alternative possible explanations of the dynamics in the case.

When employing QCA, researchers make a series of decisions that can impact the results of their analysis, and these need to be transparent to allow others to judge the robustness of the results. This chapter has discussed QCA and offered an example-based guideline that addresses how to discuss one's selection of conditions, calibration, and simplifying assumptions and other choices made.

Notes

1 Parsimony in research methodology and theory refers to aiming toward simplicity by avoiding overtly complex explanations or theories of causality that are difficult to replicate or inspect. One should not make explanatory models too complex if it is not necessary; rather, the aim should be to provide as simple an explanation as possible. In practice, from a methodological perspective, one should utilize, develop, and create theories that are simpler and focus attention on a limited number of cases or instances that are observed at the end of the research process, that is, a more delimited data set that is drawn from the bulk of the research material. Parsimony also means having fewer explanatory factors or outcomes that are analyzed (Aarts 2007). QCA has typically been used to strive toward parsimony, in the sense that it starts with a broad set of possible causal explanatory factors and outcomes and then in a step-by-step process eliminates those cases that do not seem to be so important. This process is in support of working toward a "minimal formula" or a solution that is as simple as possible. However, QCA, and especially some strands and applications of QCA, differs from other methods in that it makes space and allows for multiple causations to be explored and used in explanations, instead of favoring broad

and "coarse," simple general theories across blunt categories. This is in contrast to the claims in comparative political economy, which could use a country as the unit of analysis, and the outcome or explanatory factor (and theory) could be as broad as democracy or industrial capitalism. In this book, I will demonstrate how to work toward a parsimonious explanation for a very complex, real-world situation, and I also offer an alternative to this kind of parsimony-seeking strategy by explaining and illustrating the real-world problems that can arise if overt parsimony-seeking is favored at the cost of trying to explain the actual dynamics and factors of importance in the situation in question.

2 I am grateful to Charles Ragin for pointing out the variety of uses that fsQCA has, making the criticism of fsQCA from the dynamics of contention perspective unwarranted (personal communication, December 31, 2020).
3 Extractivism has emerged in the past 15 years as an important concept to analyze raw material extractions that are largely export-focused and environmentally highly destructive. An analysis through the extractivism lens places importance on observing the ideas, policies, and practices behind these natural resource extractions (see Kröger 2020).
4 Map produced May 16, 2013, by the author with the assistance of Jenni Munne; mapping of project areas based on field research in 2012–2013. Map boundaries downloaded from d-maps.com/carte.php?num_car=24855.
5 Map produced by the author (with help from Jenni Munne); map boundaries downloaded from http://d-maps.com/carte.php?num_car=24875&lang=en.
6 See http://conflitosambientaismg.lcc.ufmg.br/observatorio-de-conflitos-ambientais/mapa-dos-conflitos-ambientais/ (accessed August 15, 2015).
7 Carlos Bittencourt from IBASE argued in our interview—*before* the massive tailings dam catastrophe—that the Alegria mine has the world's largest tailings pond, whose water use is very badly supervised.
8 www.mining-technology.com/features/featurethe-worlds-11-biggest-iron-ore-mines-4180663/ (accessed August 15, 2015).
9 For the grievances, see www.ifch.unicamp.br/profseva/SEVA_texto%20analiticoR_MapeamentoGESTA_junho2011.pdf (accessed August 15, 2015).
10 See http://conflitosambientaismg.lcc.ufmg.br/conflito/?id=241 (accessed August 15, 2015).

2 Studying complex interactions and outcomes
Selecting key factors in social movement studies

Chapter Abstract: *This chapter introduces the key factors and conditions that are used as analytical frameworks for the QCA application in this book. The chapter details several important factors that should be considered in an analysis and why, with a focus on explaining how certain factors can be crafted as heuristic devices in studying complex interactions. These include factors related to different resistance strategies, government actions and roles, geographic contingencies, and the actions of corporations and third parties, in addition to the contextual features of the studied polities. This chapter explains how the focus of attention and delimitation of the studied phenomena can potentially affect the study results. In addition, I will explore the benefits of focusing on a specific set of issues, such as resource politics and political ecology in a sectorial manner, rather than making overtly generalized claims based on a blurred database with multiple issues under consideration. This helps in the crucial task of explaining and showing how to calibrate data, that is, how to get from qualitative data to QCA.*

Data calibration, that is, how to get from qualitative data (especially ethnographic data) to QCA, has not been discussed enough in the literature thus far. However, the issue is crucial, and I will discuss in this chapter how complex interactions can be rendered into causal conditions that can be assessed via QCA. This process is demonstrated through a two-pronged approach, where causal factors and outcomes are identified both through theoretical literatures and empirical realities, juxtaposing and merging lessons from prior scholarship on particular and pertinent topics, and through the personal experiences a field researcher accrues when visiting new areas and getting to know new realities. I think that this process, based on both induction and deduction, is essential for getting at more interesting and robust causal conditions.

The starting point for my journey with using QCA-type thinking was at the University of California, Berkeley, in 2008, when my thesis supervisor,

Peter Evans, recommended that I get to know Charles Ragin's QCA method. Evans suggested that this method could be used to organize and systematically study the many pulp conflict and investment cases I had covered for my PhD dissertation. By that point, I had conducted field research across most Brazilian pulp investment areas and visited similar paper pulp ventures elsewhere in South America and in Finland. I had a thesis draft of over 300 pages; however, it was too elaborate, going here and there, having deep theoretical discussions, and also covering more sporadically the 14 pulp investment cases around Brazil that I investigated.

Another suggestion I received while studying sociology at UC Berkeley was that I expand the focus of my work to include the theories of social movement studies and to engage in discussions with professors who worked in that field. It was also recommended that I get to know the work on dynamics of contention by Doug McAdam, Sid Tarrow, and Charles Tilly. My theory base thus far had reached far and wide, and I needed to further focus the key theoretical contribution. Heeding this advice, I started going through the social movement literature in more detail, systematically even, focusing primarily on that theory, using other theorists as helpful side theories or background theorists for specific uses.

Social movement studies, particularly the strand of contentious politics research, sees complex phenomena, like conflicts and their outcomes, as a result of the interplay between contesters, targets, and the state (McAdam, Tarrow, and Tilly 2001, 2008). The actions of states, governments, movements, targets, and third parties should be studied as parts of the broader political dynamics (Luders 2010). The core of the theoretical contribution that I wanted to utilize and advance was formed by two distinct strands of literature. The first was the dynamics of contention approach (McAdam, Tarrow, and Tilly 2001, 2008),while the second was the study of investment politics (McAdam and Boudet 2012) The phenomena I studied were very complex, and I needed a theory that could address this complexity and provide a theoretical framework to organize the data. Both of these approaches are based on the study of very complex phenomena, where it is understood that there are different social mechanisms and processes that explain outcomes and that should be the focus of attention. Thus, I looked for mechanisms and processes that would provide explanations for the particular research hypothesis that I used to organize my data gathering and reporting. This hypothesis was that a well-organized social movement, using particular strategies, can counter corporate resource exploitation, even in difficult circumstances. It is important to have a guiding hypothesis or research question, with subhypotheses, to be able to start to decipher and delineate the causal conditions for QCA. QCA is particularly helpful when there are several factors that together can be seen as causing certain outcomes.

McAdam, Tarrow, and Tilly (2001) theorize several generalizable mechanisms of contention. I thought that such mechanisms could be analyzed for their presence and activeness via csQCA. This could help in addressing the issue of causality, as McAdam, Tarrow, and Tilly (2001) do not make causal claims about the mechanisms and their outcomes. Besides addressing causality, I wanted to assess how particular relations between the state and movements, or between movements and corporations (without state mediation), affected the outcomes. Most conflict dynamics revolve around state mediation, but when it comes to investment politics where globalizing corporations are often key players, an increasing part do not. I built on the work of Soule (2009), who provides an analysis of the role of politics outside state mediation (private politics) for economic outcomes, by carving out a particular causal condition to analyze how the use of the strategy choice of private dialogues to reach a private deal with corporations influences economic and political outcomes across different cases.

The choice to use QCA also flowed from demands in movement scholarship. I followed the suggestion of prior studies (e.g., Cress and Snow 2000) to analyze the ways in which different causal conditions influence movement outcomes. I understood that this could provide a more far-reaching analysis than research that focuses on a single mechanism, such as framing, or an approach that pits differing approaches against each other, such as agency and structure. I pursued an analysis that could shed light on the complex, causal interrelationships that exist between strategies, dynamics, and outcomes. QCA thus became interwoven as a method for a broader exercise of theory-building.

I wanted to observe different types of outcomes, as their simultaneous analysis surfaced in the data as necessary and in the literature as a gap. In the scholarship on movement outcomes, most research had focused on political outcomes (Amenta et al. 2010). However, an emerging line of scholarship, which studied social movements and their influence on investment and economic outcomes, was being built at the time when I created my theoretical framework (e.g., Borras and Franco 2013; King 2008; King and Soule 2007; McAdam and Boudet 2012; Sherman 2011; Soule 2009; Vasi 2009). These scholars demanded, in particular, further study of the causalities between protest and business within the dynamics of contention (see Kröger 2020). Starting with this premise, I redesigned my PhD data in 2008 and finished my thesis on the role of social movements in Brazilian pulp investments in 2010 (Kröger 2010). After that, I wanted to explore whether a similar set of strategies and dynamics also applied in another country context and sector. I began to compare Brazil with India and forestry with mining. After conducting field research on mining between 2010 and 2013, I returned to writing QCA based on the results. I saw what new theories had been created and integrated them, while going back and forth between my new and old data, and I kept up to date with the new scholarship. This process took many years, until 2020.

It is important to reflect on one's own position and process of knowledge creation and on how one's findings do and do not resonate with other scholars' findings. After I finished the bulk of the field research by 2014, other publications came out that could be used for retrospective reflection on what to focus on in my data set, for example, identifying the novelties and key contributions therein. Giugni and Grasso (2015) stated in their study of (environmental) social movements that too little is known about the interplay between the local and global levels and about movements' impacts in general. Lu and Tao (2017) argued that studying the diversity of roles and strategies of resistance groups was a research avenue that needed undertaking. Reviews of Latin American studies of social movements found that in the 2010s, a focus on movement strategies surfaced as a key feature and contribution when the publications cross-referenced Latin American realities with the theories of contentious politics, which thus far had come mostly from the Global North (Krausova 2020). In retrospect, the finding of the centrality of strategies for advancing movement scholarship was in line with what I had found in the 2000s, when cross-referencing my own experiences working within the realities of rural Latin American with the dynamics of contention research approach. By this I mean, the reality on the ground highlighted the importance of paying attention to key movement strategies and their interactions with states, corporations, and the other varied political games (Kröger 2010, 2013, 2020). More broadly, the Latin American study of social movements situates these interactions as symptoms and agents of the wider societal changes than is found in studies emanating from North America (Bringel 2019). QCA applications need to consider these different perspectives and realities when selecting factors and outcomes, opening findings through broader discussions, and drawing conclusions. Considering these gaps that the movement literature identified, my data became more relevant; I already had data that addressed these gaps, and my data formed a cross-contextual comparison.

QCA helps in seeking solutions for complex phenomena, and there are some important questions to ask in this process. The key questions one needs to ask in QCA include the following. What is the key outcome that one is interested in and wants to investigate further? What is the dependent variable that one wants to explain? Why does that matter? The selection of this outcome does not need to reflect one's own opinion, but it can guide attention to important issues.

I was interested in shedding more light on the dynamics that explain outcomes related to investment politics, both political and economic outcomes.

In support of this goal, I adopted three economic and four political outcomes as dependent variables. I placed the most attention on studying where, when, and how the economic outcome of all discontinued mines or projects occurred (EO1). This was the key outcome I was interested in, and the other six outcomes were specific instances related to this outcome. I also noted the causal condition complexes that led to a significant curtailment in the extraction volume (EO2) and a deceleration of expansion (EO3). These all addressed the existing research gap related to how movements affect economic outcomes. Regarding political outcomes, I observed when resistance spread transnationally, based on regionally situated mobilizations (PO1), and when armed revolutionary agency was created and spread (PO4). However, these are just examples; I also studied other types of political outcomes (see Table 3.3 for details). This observation was included because I already had the data gathered via my field research and because otherwise this rich data would have been lost and not been reported for all the cases, as the process of publication demands parsimony, particularly in most approaches to QCA and in academic publishing in general. However, I will first focus on providing basic tables and truth tables that display the data in a revealing way instead of pursuing parsimony, as suggested by Collier (2014). Important data can be conceived in the QCA tables that are then used later to form truth tables to look for all kinds of causalities, as the next chapter will illustrate. With the political outcomes, I wanted to answer the call for a better understanding of how armed and nonarmed resistance affects outcomes and how movement resistance is related to the creation of particular types of political agency, on different scales, such as the global scale.

The resistance strategies I crafted as heuristic tools to be analyzed were mostly based on prior research that identified many of them as being important factors to explain when and how industrial tree plantations do or do not expand in Brazil and elsewhere (Kröger 2013). These strategies were lightly fine-tuned to better fit the realities of the existing resistance to mining, and more resistance strategies were added for systematic comparison as these surfaced in the data collection. The most notable of these were armed resistance strategies and private politics. I then assessed whether other factors from the vast database could be placed within the Boolean logic of csQCA that could explain in complementary terms or even better the outcomes rather than the strategies.

The logic behind looking for contingency factors that might explain the investment politics around iron ore mining was based on an exploration of factors specific to this industry, as one cannot meaningfully compare, for example, gold and bauxite mining conflicts because their dynamics vary so radically due to differing extraction styles, markets, and value webs with different actors. Therefore, it would be even less meaningful to look for possible explanatory factors from studies on resistance to completely different sectors outside of mining, such as general resistance struggles against resource investments in India or Brazil. A big problem with many prior studies on extractivism has been their focus on it as a general process, although in even one specific subsector, such as iron ore extraction, there are crucial differences in investment style and pace (e.g., based on them being mostly open-pit or underground operations) with huge impacts on potential political dynamics and investment outcomes.

With several contexts included, complexity increases, and too much complexity makes it difficult to analyze the most interesting interactions. As I had many contextual differences, it was best to focus my attention on a specific sector to rule out the possibility of sectoral specificities: I first studied large-scale, paper pulp investments and then new iron ore mining expansion via open-pit mines. I would recommend a similar precise focus on subsectors and extraction styles to rule out possible methodological problems later, such as having factors affect issues that are not controlled for. This is currently plausible and important because as economic sectors are ever more globalized, changes in one part of the world affect the whole sector at a global level. The focus on investment politics research needs to cover the key sectors that affect each other. Similar questions around how to bound the key research subject need to be carefully considered before and during research projects to obtain meaningful data and focus.

Because the logic of csQCA does not allow all ethnographic or broader structural observations to be turned into Boolean logic, the exercise included here has its limitations. For example, complex contextual and historical reasons, such as variance across differing subnational governance systems and agrarian social structures, that might well influence the outcomes are better explored through other styles of presenting research, such as political ethnographic texts. This is a limitation of the method.[1]

In this light, this book illustrates how QCA can be used, in spite of these limitations, to make a much broader analysis across all the relevant (major iron ore mines) cases, with no major or relevant nonobserved cases, and thus provide an important methodological triangulation. This is helpful to ensure that the narrative-style ethnographic accounts do not end up inadvertently leaving behind important outlier cases, or cases that are not considered as central by the analyst who does not systematically review all of the cases based on the best available data that could be attained at a given time but instead relies on showcasing some illustrative cases. Furthermore, as I will discuss, detailed and careful QCA typically results in gaining major new insights, and writing the ethnographic accounts in a different way allows outlier cases and common features to reveal important overall differences and generalities.

Case selection is always a very tricky exercise, which is why data sets with no nonobserved cases should figure more prominently in research. There will be trade-offs in this, as it will not be possible for one researcher to conduct extensive field research across all the cases in a medium-n set (I studied over 20 cases) or to collect as much data on all the cases. However, the researcher should do their utmost to go through the best available data on each case and then use this as the basis for making a systematic study. Otherwise, one runs the serious risk of focusing only on the pivotal cases, assuming that they represent the whole state of affairs in a given sector or issue, while the truth can be far more complex and nuanced. Of course, one can start from a smaller data set, and this is how I would recommend proceeding. One can begin from a shared polity, context, and sector and then increase the scale of observation to new contexts within the same polity and sector (e.g., from one Brazilian state to the whole country, in one sector of investment). This kind of smaller, comprehensive study can then be used as a basis by other researchers to find all the cases that should be studied in more detail in a given sector or issue area and engage in deeper analyses of these elsewhere around the world. Then, the initial QCA truth tables can be revisited and revised, if needed, on the basis of the new accumulated knowledge. The totality of the cases, although messier, can be presented by QCA and used over and over again by the author and other researchers to dig out interesting subcases and causal paths for deeper inspection through process tracing or ethnographic accounts.

To identify key explanatory factors for QCA, one should also draw on studies about the specific sector and broader issues. I canvassed the mining and natural resource conflict literatures to see what else to observe. If possible, what is missing from prior research or is presented as arbitrary results should especially be included. Much attention in the literature on mining conflicts has been paid to explaining where, when, why, or how resistance occurs (e.g., Arsel, Hogenboom, and Pellegrini 2016; Bebbington and Bury 2013; Dougherty and Olsen 2014; Haslam and Tanimoune 2016) and to resistance networking and state and corporate responses (e.g., Arce 2014; Broad and Cavanagh 2015; Conde 2017). The causes of conflict have been studied; for example, Conde (2017) takes a global view on how and why communities resist mining through a review of more than 200 publications, while Haslam and Tanimoune (2016) focus on mining conflict determinants in Latin America utilizing a quantitative analysis based on 640 cases. The shortfalls in qualitative approaches and particularly case studies as suggested by Haslam and Tanimoune (2016) can be answered via QCA. The shortfalls mentioned include the need for hypothesis testing, a better case selection technique, variance across dependent variables, and the adoption of comparative approaches.

When conducting statistical analyses to explore the possible correlations between almost 350 mining cases around the world, Özkaynak et al. (2015, 49) could not discover "when a disruptive project will be stopped;" however, the database and analysis herein provide some findings on when temporal cessations (that is, the discontinuations of mining or projects within the studied period) occurred in the contexts of Brazilian and Indian iron ore projects. Furthermore, I do not aim to make broadly generalizable assertions on the basis of this database as it focuses on one subsector in regions that only present a fraction of two countries' geographical territories and subregional political dynamics. However, the cases studied here do provide fresh and new contributions to different literatures on the aforementioned and other topics (movement outcomes, rising global powers, mining, etc.). Through this data set, I provide one cross-continental analysis of resistance upsurge causalities, which is a key research gap in the mining literature identified by Conde (2017).

Identifying and exploring the role of key social movement strategies

Brazil and India provide a mix of sufficient similarity and disparity in contexts, state and government structures and actions, extraction models, local political dynamics, and resistance strategies. However, there is a major difference between the two, as large parts of India have armed resource conflicts; the mining and resistance politics in these regions are strongly embedded in being influenced by and creating such contexts. This disparity makes it possible to compare the effectiveness of similar strategies in differing contexts.

I unite the study of armed resistance groups and contexts with peaceful movements [an approach called for by McAdam, Tarrow, and Tilly (2001) and Lu and Tao (2017)]. Armed resistance comes in many forms, as does its subcategory, armed revolutionary agency. In India, armed revolutionary resistance relies on the actual use of arms to incite revolution in a particular Maoist sense (where insurgents garner support particularly as a result of the deep grievances of rural and forest populations targeted by extractive capital, such as Adivasis) (Banerjee 2013; Choudhary 2012) or to secede from the state to form an ethnically separate region (Karlsson 2011). I distinguish such nuances in the types of actions addressing extractivism as different resistance strategies, as they might result in different political and economic outcomes.

Studies on the economic outcomes of many different types of protest activities (including violent and armed) need to offer process- and mechanism-based explanations rather than just comparing conditions (Bosi and Giugni 2012). My finding challenged the conventional thinking about the power of arms. I found that, in many cases, nonviolent direct action has the potential to lead to even more profound economic impacts than armed resistance. However, in many other cases, armed and peaceful resistance strategies were present in the same area, which makes it imperative to observe in detail the minute differences in strategy sets and outcomes across such cases to be able to identify or at least draw some conclusions about the roles of armed and peaceful resistance as separate paths.

The material consists of 23 cases, which are assessed via QCA to define the necessary and sufficient causal conditions related to both political and economic outcomes. Seven outcome varieties are studied for variations across 22 causal conditions and their complexes in the 23 cases. I analyze how the context of resistance organization influences the outcomes, such as having middle-class support. I also assess the potential influence of corporate agency differences and geographic factors, such as ore content. This research strategy offers a rigorous test for the initial working hypothesis that five key resistance strategies can explain investment outcomes and serves to reveal if, when, and how these outcomes occur.

My comparative apparatus was built to study the roles of different types of resistance strategies together with the differences in the local political contexts and contingency factors in the investment areas. In the next chapter, I will show how I first explored whether the simultaneous use of these five key strategies can generally explain when resistance discontinues resource extraction (see Kröger 2013, 2020):[2]

a   Organizing and politicizing a mass social movement;
b   campaigning under a nonmodernist framing;
c   protesting peacefully and physically so that this action is noted, for example, by blocking important resource export routes;
d   networking; and
e   embedding the state in electoral, institutional, and/or judicial politics while retaining autonomy.

The QCA tables presented in Chapter 3 will also summarize the outcomes, strategies, and contextual differences and similarities and identify several key parameters that should be considered in studies of investment politics in general and in studies on the sociopolitical dimensions of extractive industries in particular. The findings suggest that, in general, the use of several resistance strategies is more likely to lead to the outcomes desired by the resistance. Similar outcomes, such as the discontinuation of mining projects, can be obtained through multiple pathways. However, the most secure pathway to attain impressive outcomes seems to be the use all five of the strategies outlined previously and the avoidance of private and armed politics.

There are good reasons for separating these five different resistance strategies. I created these strategies as heuristic tools informed by extensive fieldwork across different resistance movements and conflict situations in investment areas since 2004 and by literature reviews of the existing studies on social movement outcomes, from which key factors were identified, tested through QCA rounds, and refined. For a detailed description of how the strategy set was developed, see Kröger (2010, 2011, 2013, 2020). A summary follows. This kind of explanation should be offered to outline what each QCA factor observes, covers, and purports to be causing and why it is included.

Strategy a specifically involves mass social movement organizations but does not include resistance that is organized by NGOs. This allows for observation of whether a mass social movement organization is needed to make a difference in the resistance efforts. As an example, I use the Brazilian Landless Rural Workers' Movement (MST), which is known as Latin America's key mass movement with 1.5 million members. In mining politics, the MST has been among the most important resistance actors protesting against Vale and iron ore extraction in Brazil and helping to form specific mining-focused networks, NGOs, and movements, both nationally and globally. The MST is a good example of strategy a, as this movement has an established organizational structure with a large base, specified sectors, and regional (unofficial) administrative bodies created by the social movement organization. This is not a movement that is either loose or imagined by researchers or in campaign framings; it is a real-world movement with a large membership and with which people identify. This also is not an NGO but a social movement, which means being part of the movement with one's life in fuller terms than in NGOs, where the workers are NGO specialists, who are typically paid and who might often be very dedicated but whose numbers are much more limited than in mass movements.

Normative struggles around the framing of what an economic activity is—for example, mining—and what it does are essential factors in explaining investment politics and their outcomes. Therefore, I study the role of campaigning using heterodox, nonmodernist, anti-mining framing (strategy b), which fundamentally challenges turning nature into monetarily valued and globally commensurable "natural resources" meant for use in processes of commodification [more precisely, meant for anthropocentric use in ontologies and processes of commodification; see Kröger (2020) for a detailed discussion]. Mining conflicts are often (but not always, as the QCA will reveal) struggles whereby heterodox frames challenge the established order and are adopted more generally as the depiction of mining, for example, as "socioenvironmental havoc" and/or "criminal activity" rather than as "development." In their review of studies that use this particular framing perspective—similar to my study, which focuses on explaining political or economic outcomes—Snow et al. (2014, 35) argue that how activists frame their core claims has "a decisive impact on building movements, winning positive outcomes, and shaping the overall trajectories of movement efforts." I explore whether this is the case by analyzing the presence of strategy b.

Not all resistance groups or even social movements protest in all the different cases in which they are involved, not even against the same company or the same investment model across the board. Thus, it is necessary to disaggregate protesting (c) as a specific strategy that might be in operation in some investment project cases and areas, but not in others. It is sometimes understood that social movements would always, by definition, include at least protesting (c) and networking (d). However, my results show that this is not always necessarily the case. Some local resistance groups are networked, while others are not. In addition, despite being massive, formal organizations with a name, some discreet movements either are limited to a locale or are against one specific investment project, at least at their outset. It is possible that later on they do start to network (d) with people, movements, and other entities in other locations.

Strategy e is subdivided into e1–e3; however, this strategy generally refers to a situation where the resistance is embedding the state in electoral, institutional, and/or judicial politics while retaining autonomy. In this strategy, electoral (e1), institutional (e2), and judicial politics (e3) are distinguished as subcategories of state embedding styles.[3] Here, I flip the concept of embedded autonomy by Evans (1995) to analyze the role that civil society actors can have in influencing the state.

The reason for disaggregating a–e and even the three subcategories for strategy e is that, while some of them might seem to be quite similar or even seem to be overlapping strategies or categories of social movements, they are not used by the resistance (or even one single resistance group) in all the investment cases in which they are involved. If we lump together some or all of the preceding strategies under "social movements," we cannot disaggregate and analyze important differences, which becomes crucial particularly when studying the reasons for the outcomes of investment politics at the project level. This reasoning is based on a multi-case-study logic.

My prior study found that the use of a strategy set very similar to the preceding five strategies was the both necessary and sufficient condition for at least slowing down, or even discontinuing, the expansion of tree plantations that were established with the aim of building large pulp mills in the investment areas in question (Kröger 2010, 2011, 2013). The research design in that prior study was similar to that used as an example of the QCA application herein. It was based on QCA, however, it focused mostly on Brazil and all its pulp investment projects between 1990 and 2010. In this study, a different commodity and economic sector, a comparison between two large countries, and the inclusion of armed conflict contexts enable the maximization of the pressure under which the findings on resistance strategy causalities are placed. As Tavory and Timmermans (2013, 708) argue, the use of multiple variations in the data set "provides insight into the regularity and unfolding of the process" and makes it possible to make stronger processual causal claims.

To grasp the totality of possibly important factors, I also observed the presence of three other resistance strategies, which offer alternative and competing explanations. While resistance may be using one or several of the preceding strategies that clearly challenge extractivism, less clearly confrontational strategies may also be used by the resistance. This type of less confrontational strategy was categorized in my study as strategy f, which is the participation in private politics initiatives of companies with the aim of reaching an agreement directly with the corporations without state mediation [e.g., corporate social responsibility (CSR)]. If strategy f occurred, this meant that the movements received some material or monetary compensation from the company and/or state actors involved. Thus, the database also includes the important factor of compensation and its relation to the outcome of physically influencing the extraction pace and style (which are my key dependent variables), either directly in the given investment area (economic outcomes) or indirectly by expanding political willingness to resist mining that is also occurring elsewhere in that time or some other potential future time (political outcomes).

I also studied whether armed revolutionary resistance (g1) was present or whether the threat of resistance by arms was explicit but no violence took place (g2), as the role of violence in influencing movement outcomes is still unclear and mixed in the literature (see, e.g., Bosi and Giugni 2012). The QCA tables will make it possible to observe whether strategies a–g produce mutually supporting causal condition complexes (leading to mining discontinuations) or whether some of them work against the goals of resistance and the other strategies' power.

Conditions affecting movement strategies: the role of contingencies and other actors

The study of strategies alone, even all possible strategies, may not capture the full picture. Prior scholarship on movements has shown that there is no clear or straightforward causality running from grievances to mobilization and outcomes. The set of resistance strategies used is just one explanation for investment outcomes, as there are certainly other factors that have an influence. It is also important to study resistance, the state, and capital in a dynamic, relational way. This leads to an understanding of the dynamics of contention, where the crucial factors include the kind of state and capital addressed, that is, the role of corporate agency with its case-specific interests (Kröger 2013). Baviskar (2001) illustrates that the contrast in the success of two resistance groups against large-scale investment projects in India may best be explained by variation in the nature of the state and capital they address (Baviskar is able to make this claim as she controlled for the type of resistance: they had similar class and membership bases and similar tactics for building interclass alliances). Prior theoretical-empirical findings (based on cases in the West) have also emphasized the effects of variation on outcomes between targets and third parties (Luders 2010) and between issues (Giugni 2004); higher level issues crucial for the targets or third parties are harder to influence.[4] In Baviskar's (2001) Indian cases, the less successful group posed a threat to relatively immobile political and economic capital; its growing strength in the land conflict studied signified a direct undermining of vested interests in the area that had nowhere else to go. Thus, counterresistance was harsh, and resistance was unsuccessful. The second group attained their goals because their target was a more mobile project funded by national-international investment capital, for whom the land in dispute was just one of many possible investment localities. In this view, corporate agency and the contextual dynamics strongly influence the outcomes of resistance.

Prior theoretical-empirical findings (based on cases in the West) have also emphasized the effects of variation between issues on outcomes (Giugni 2004); higher level issues crucial for the targets or third parties are harder to influence. Using this understanding as the basis, I set out to observe via field research whether and how corporate agency and contextual dynamics influence the outcomes of resistance. I explored the role of important contingencies to track down when and how strategies a–g are related to certain outcomes and when (in the presence of which other causal conditions and explanatory factors) they are not. The contingency factors (listed in Tables 3.7 and 3.8 in Chapter 3) were selected and formulated for a comparative examination on the basis of the prior literature review and repeated rounds of QCA across the cases. The centrality of the five key strategies was further tested by exposing the database to competing explanations.

The purpose of the contingencies part of the QCA is to introduce and explore factors that I had reason to suspect could affect or could be seen to affect the outcomes. For example, I looked at the role played by geography, such as the presence of hilly forests, comparing a *geographic factor* that strongly correlates with the presence of hilly forests in the tropics: High-quality ore (over 60% average iron content) (GE1). One reason why I focused on iron ore and not all mining is that doing so makes it possible to observe the finite differences possibly caused by the commodity extracted. I assess the role of iron's voluminous particularity; iron ore is one of the world's bulkiest commodities, which might seriously affect its political economy and conflict dynamics. The 60% iron content is an important threshold within the industry, as it marks the difference between more and less valuable ore. Ore suitable for use in different steel-making processes should thus be considered as a potential explanation for how a similar set of strategies might produce differing outcomes, because the miners are keener to hold on to their more valuable resource or established commodity chains. This type of analysis is fruitful in providing answers to structure-agency debates, that is, whether the kind of strategies (agency) used by resistance is more important than the setting in which they take place. I determined that contextual features do play major roles in defining how the strategies work, but that the iron ore content was not one of the key features; rather, it could be ruled out. Much more important was the presence or absence of civil war and armed-conflict-type resource extraction settings; their presence often correlated with the presence of ethnic minorities as the key actors resisting the expansion. Another important factor was whether the investment area in question was located on a country's primary resource frontier. Such areas are often considered peripheral and key sources of appropriation (such as the Carajás region in the eastern Amazon and Chhattisgarh in India) and, therefore, face much more violence and state-corporate pressure than areas closer to the core areas of these countries (such as Goa in India and Minas Gerais key cities in Brazil). To the extent possible, I identified several contingency and contextual factors based on ethnographic and other material for systematic csQCA. Most of the contextual features, or features of the differing polities and political economies, were not rendered into Boolean logic but were analyzed structurally and institutionally. In QCA proper, the focus is on providing a study of some potentially important contingency factors in order to examine whether they played a role and should be studied more in detail. As QCA is a widely applicable method, the cases I covered could also be marked for their contextual differences in a more parsimonious way (e.g., whether the case had an armed conflict or not); however, I considered it crucial to break these quite blunt contextual characterizations into processes and mechanisms to avoid a structure-agency dichotomy. Thus, I assessed, for example, the presence of armed resistance agency, which is also shorthand for understanding that there is an armed conflict context.

With similar attention focused on turning structural explanations into more agentive and dynamic conditions, I compared several different social settings and drew from this exploration three *specificities in the context of resistance organization* (factors a1–a3). I analyzed how the investment outcomes vary when local middle-classes largely supported resistance (a1); the key resistance group included urban, middle-class professionals in key positions (a2); and/or several cross-class, interethnic, or intersector resistance groups were present (a3).

These are broad categories as they were evaluated as either 1 or 0 on the basis of field research observations, interviews with experts, and triangulation from secondary material of different sorts. It is important in QCA to open the thresholds of observation protocols and be prepared to be able to give justified and longer accounts for the value given to each case, if asked. It could be argued with confidence that the middle classes have largely supported the resistance (a1 = 1), for example, in the Apolo and Mina del Rey cases in Minas Gerais, Brazil, but not in the cases of Keonjhar or Minas-Rio wherein the resistance consisted primarily of social underdogs. Middle-class professionals helped the resistance in Casa da Pedra, in Congonhas (a2 = 1); these were mining engineers who joined the resistance movement. Goa exhibited the situation of having several different, largely caste-separated resistance movements (a3 = 1), while in Keonjhar it was the Adivasis who were resisting (a3 = 0). To provide the detailed stories of the reasons for giving the values across the 23 cases for all 22 causal factors and 7 outcomes would take far too much space, which is why it is reasonable to focus only on the ones that reveal the general or important or the anomalous causal paths. However, each case should be carefully analyzed, so that the valuation given for it in QCA can be justified.

Contexts need to be disaggregated into the factors that compose them, factors that should also be agentive if possible, because agency is real and tractable as it takes place via actions while structures are often latent or mere potentials. As the role of third parties has been shown in prior research to be of key importance (Luders 2010), I disaggregate two, *third-party roles* that surfaced as possibly important for subsequent comparative scrutiny. These were, broadly, tourism, agriculture, or other significant mining-critical entrepreneurs present (T1) and ore that went or would go primarily to China (T2).[5] While China was not a direct actor in these conflicts, its role was important as a key destination of iron ore from many sites, which meant that the Indian and Brazilian states had different strategic reasons to possibly curb such extractions (a boon to local resistance aims of discontinuing these operations). These are also factors of great interest to global development scholars, and their inclusion makes it possible to examine whether the presence of foreign governments in international trade (particularly with China) might delimit resistance success (or whether their presence has no notable impact).

48 *Studying complex interactions and outcomes*

I also look at the *composition of capital*, whether it is dispersed or united and private or public, and what difference this aspect might make (see Table 3.1 for a list of the mining companies active in each case). Additionally, I introduce a set of *corporate agency differences* whose presence and influence as causal conditions are compared across all the cases via QCA: Underestimation of the resistance potential by the targets (CD1); the size of the company(ies) [1 = large, 0 = small (CD2)];[6] and sophisticated corporate countertactics to curb mobilization (CD3).

I also isolate three factors detailing the *political role* and *type of target* for systematic analysis: Primarily central-government-led expansion (P1); a primary national resource frontier (P2); and a deep ethnic injustice, that is, mining that represents a profound ethnic injustice by benefiting mostly elite ethnic groups and perpetrating forestland loss that affects mostly vulnerable communities (e.g., indigenous groups) (P3). The presence of these causal conditions is compared across all 22 investment cases to see whether there is a relation between these conditions and the political and economic outcomes.

Next, I will present the findings of the QCA, which illustrate how one can write a condensed analysis of a large database and which looks for patterns of causalities across many causal factors and outcomes throughout the cases. After this, I will discuss in more detail the roles of some of contingencies and causal paths because, in the face of the complexity of the contextual factors, it is helpful to highlight specific (groups of) cases in terms of predominant and alternative causal accounts.

Notes

1 I have addressed this limitation in my broader research project by writing an ethnographic and context-analyzing account of the data, including many factors left outside of the QCA performed here, that can be found in other publications (see, e.g., Kröger 2019, 2020) or is still forthcoming, as I have plenty of material and analyses on these cases that have not yet been published.
2 Please note that I do not follow the QCA algorithm convention of capitalization of the causal conditions in their abbreviated form. This is because I generally agree that too extensive "algorithmizing" of the QCA method is a problem.
3 In terms of organizational analysis, it can be said that once embedding has occurred, vertical linkages between the societal and state sides of collective action have been created, showing that what Lu and Tao (2017, 1762) call "weak bridging ties" in vertical state-society relations are important conduits in exercising political influence.
4 The issue at stake matters. A key issue is sunk costs, both in investment politics and particularly in mining. Resistance generally had the target of curbing the rampant mining booms, but the booms have varied regionally and, thus, the target has not been the same everywhere. In some places it has been easier than

Studying complex interactions and outcomes 49

in others. For example, Anglo-American's Minas-Rio project in Conceição de Mato Dentro (Minas Gerais) was given a license to operate on September 29, 2014. This license was issued despite several irregularities and local resistance. However, this company was a hard target for the resistance because the company already had the world's largest ore pipeline—from Minas Gerais to Rio de Janeiro—which it could not use elsewhere. Ironically, the ore has proven to be of lesser quality than expected. This suggests that geographical considerations or factor endowments do not determine investment outcomes as much as one would expect [see Watts (2004) and Nugent and Robinson (2010) for similar analyses], while politics and sunk costs do seem to be central factors. The company pushed the project through in spite of the hurdles, as it had already invested so much [www.theguardian.com/business/2016/feb/16/anglo-american-plans-to-hasten-coal-and-iron-ore-sell-offs-as-profits-halve (accessed March 30, 2016)].

5 The threshold for identifying a case as having T2 active was that over half of the ore went to China and for T1 that there was a clearly identifiable industry that would had been negatively affected by open-pit iron ore mining in the investment area and that had openly voiced criticism against the project. This was the case, for example, in Kudremukh (agriculture), Salem (textile industry), and Goa (tourism), but not in Keonjhar or Carajás (which were cast as resource peripheries and where I did not find evidence of a competing industry being present or critical of mining).

6 There were only four investment areas in the database that had small companies (CD2 = 0) as the key, proximate extractive actors. These included, for example, the Bellary area, where the extraction was mostly carried out by unknown mining mafias consisting of state ministers, and Kudremukh, where the small-size, state-owned iron ore company KIOCL Limited was doing the extraction. In the other cases, the investment areas had the presence of global multinationals, such as Vale, or large national state or private corporations, such as the Steel Authority of India Limited (SAIL) corporation in Rowghat.

3 How to apply QCA? An illustration through a QCA of investment politics outcomes in Brazil and India

Chapter Abstract: *This chapter will show the reader how to conduct a csQCA. One of the explanatory tools provided will be several tables that are used to link the different causal condition complexes to differing political and economic outcomes. A step-by-step analysis is presented herein, which will bring the method itself into sharp focus for other researchers to reflect on and integrate into their own research practice. This chapter is the main methodological contribution of this book. It also illustrates the type of empirical contribution that can be made with the implementation of csQCA. It uses detailed empirical findings on iron ore mining politics and the role of resistance to signpost and provide a practical example of how this method can be put into practice. It shows how QCA presents a path to conducting an analysis that is based not on isolated case studies or assumptions but rather on a rigorous and systematic analysis of social realities. This chapter illustrates a practice-based example of what type of analytical text and tables should be provided in QCA. To shed light on the methodology and how it can be used to systematically observe the separate and joint impact of various factors, this chapter is divided into two major sections, one focusing on resistance strategies and their outcomes and the other on the contingencies possibly affecting the causalities. This chapter shows how QCA can be used to explain how outcomes are produced by causal condition complexes, which in the case of social movement outcomes consists of several strategies and contingency factors. This type of analysis offers more value to policy makers and analysts than simplistic accounts of correlation. The role of necessary and sufficient causal conditions is also explored and explained through examples, alongside how to handle the recalibration of results and data gathering from a distance. I will also discuss the difference between probabilistic and minimal formula (parsimony-seeking) approaches, starting with the first approach, which makes broader reflections based on QCA tables.*

Table 3.1 summarizes the basic data on the iron mining cases in Brazil and India. I first compare the use of strategies and outcomes. After this, I study

Table 3.1 Cases studied, location, case type, main companies, and main resistance groups

Cases	State	Case type*	Main company(ies)**	Examples of involved resistance groups or platforms (if named—most were not)
India				
Goa	Goa	BF	Sesa Goa, etc.	GOA-MAP, Goa Foundation, Rainbow Warriors, Mand-Goa
Kudremukh	Karnataka	BF	KIOCL	Karnataka Vimochana Ranga (KVR), Wildlife First, ERG, KRRS
Bellary	Karnataka	BF	Obulapuram, Jindal, NMDC, etc.	SPS
Salem	Tamil Nadu	GF	(Jindal)	Kanjamalai Protection Committee, Speak Out Salem, Joint Action for Sustainable Livelihood (JASuL)
Tiruvannamalai	Tamil Nadu	GF	(Jindal)	Kavunthimalai, Vediyappanmalai Protection Committee, TNEC, DWM, DFCS, TNDAYF, WF, WC, DALM, DMK, KUMPUM, GLOW, JASuL
Joda block (Keonjhar district)	Odisha	BF	Tata, Jindal, SAIL, Essel/Birla, Bhushan, (POSCO), etc.	KIRDTI
Keonjhar (Banspal, Harichandanpur, and Telkoi blocks)	Odisha	BF	Several small companies	KIRDTI

(*Continued*)

Table 3.1 (Continued)

Cases	State	Case type*	Main company(ies)**	Examples of involved resistance groups or platforms (if named—most were not)
Khandadhar (Sundargarh)	Odisha	GF	(POSCO, KIOCL)	Khandadhar Surakhya Sangram Samiti
Pre-2005 Sundargarh (the rest of the cases in addition to Khandadhar, e.g., Koida)	Odisha	BF	Jindal, Essel, etc.	
Post-2005 Sundargarh (the rest of the cases in addition to Khandadhar, e.g., Koida)	Odisha	BF	Jindal, Essel, (POSCO), (KIOCL), etc.	
West Singhbhum	Jharkhand	BF	Tata, SAIL, (Jindal), (Mittal), etc.	CPI (Maoist)
Dantewada	Chhattisgarh	BF	NMDC (Tata), (Essar)	CPI (Maoist)
Rowghat	Chhattisgarh	GF	(Bhilai Steel Plant (BSP))	CPI (Maoist)
Manpur	Chhattisgarh	BF	Sarda/SEML, Godavari	CPI (Maoist)
Dalli Rajhara	Chhattisgarh	BF	BSP	Chattisgarh Mukti Morcha
Kawardha	Chhattisgarh	GF	(BSP)	n/a
Brazil				
Carajás (old mine) (Parauebebas)	Pará	BF	Vale, etc.	MST, Vía Campesina, MAM, indigenous movements, CPT, trade unions, Justice on Rails (JoR)
Minas-Rio (Conceição de Mato Dentro)	Minas Gerais	GF	Anglo American	Comissao Pastoral da Terra (CPT), Movimento pelas Serras e Águas de Minas, Fórum do Desenvolvimento Sustentável de Conceição do Mato Dentro

Apolo (Serra do Gandarela)	Minas Gerais	GF	Vale	Movimento pela Preservação da Serra do Gandarela, etc.
Casa de Pedra	Minas Gerais	BF	CSN	Grupo Rede Congonhas, trade union of the mine, politicians
Mina Del Rey	Minas Gerais	BF	Vale	Mariana Viva, churches, trade unions, mayor, politicians, etc.
Corumbá	Mato Grosso do Sul	BF	Vale, MMX, etc.	Kadiwéu indigenous people, Associacao Civil Ecologia e Acao (ECOA), Rede Brasileira de Justica Ambiental (RBJA)

*Case type: BF = Brownfield [existing mine(s)]; GF = Greenfield [only mining expansion project(s)].
** A company name in parentheses indicates that this key corporation intended to expand but neither it nor any other company had done so by 2015.

54 *How to apply QCA?*

the role of contingencies, which is helpful in fine-tuning the arguments and furthering their sophistication.

The impact of resistance strategies

Table 3.2 summarizes the findings about resistance strategies on a case-by-case basis. It is a helpful tool for observing whether there are shared causal condition complexes between particular sets of strategies and particular political and/or economic outcomes. Please refer to Table 3.1 for detailed information on where the cases are located. In general, in the QCA tables, 0 signifies that the strategy was not active or that an outcome was not obtained, and 1 signifies that the strategy was active or that an outcome was also present for a given causal condition complex (that is, the set of strategies influencing each local investment case).

Please note that the legend in Table 3.3 defines the abbreviations used in Table 3.2.

I first examined cases with similar outcomes and attempted to identify shared conditions to establish specific connections with the purpose of observing "whether instances of a specific outcome constitute a subset of instances of one or more causal conditions" (Rihoux 2008, 724), thereby identifying the conditions necessary for different outcomes to occur. I then used QCA to examine cases that perhaps had differing outcomes but shared causal conditions. This allowed me to observe where the simultaneous use of particular causal condition sets led. This line of inquiry provided insights into the sufficient causal conditions for differing outcomes.

Studying necessary and sufficient conditions

This section illustrates how to analyze necessary and sufficient causal conditions through an examination of the strategies that were used for blocking investment projects.

Let us start by examining major economic outcomes that did not include mine closures or project blockages (EO2). In the Casa de Pedra and Dalli Rajah examples, the resistance was not even seeking mine closures (EO1); thus, economic outcome 2 (EO2) captures a number of cases that local resistance considered victories. In the data, there are only four cases where EO2 was not an outcome (see the zeros in column EO2 in Table 3.2); thus, these anomalies or discrepancies are an excellent starting point for assessing whether resistance strategies alone can explain the outcomes. These cases are in Brazil, and the first three differ from the other cases in that their resistance is against the key projects of the world's largest miners, which are also either heavily supported by states, already have high sunk costs, or both (see Tables 3.7 and 3.8,

Table 3.2 QCA summary of findings on movement strategies

Cases	\multicolumn{10}{c}{Strategies used, active (1) or inactive (0)}								Economic outcomes			Political outcomes			
	a	b	c	d	e1	e2	e3	f	g1	g2	EO1	EO2	EO3	PO1	PO2	PO3	PO4
India																	
Goa	1	1	1	1	0	1	1	0	0	0	1	1	1	0	1	1	0
Kudremukh	1	1	1	1	0	0	1	0	0	1	1	1	1	0	0	1	0
Bellary	0	1	1	1	0	1	1	0	0	0	1	1	1	0	0	0	0
Salem	1	0	1	0	0	0	0	0	0	0	1	1	1	0	0	1	0
Tiruvannamalai	1	1	1	0	0	0	0	0	0	0	1	1	1	0	0	0	0
Joda	0	0	0	0	0	0	0	1	0	1	0	1	1	0	0	0	0
Keonjhar (Banspal, etc.)	1	1	1	1	1	1	0	0	0	0	1	1	1	0	0	0	0
Khandadhar (Sundargarh)	1	1	1	0	0	0	1	0	0	0	1	1	1	0	0	0	0
Pre-2005 Sundargarh	1	0	1	0	0	0	0	0	0	0	0	1	1	0	0	1	0
Post-2005 Sundargarh	0	0	0	0	0	0	0	0	0	0	0	1	1	0	0	0	0
West Singhbhum	1	1	1	0	0	0	0	0	0	1	1	1	1	0	0	0	1
Dantewada	1	1	1	1	0	1	0	0	1	1	1	1	1	0	0	0	1
Rowghat	1	0	1	0	0	0	0	0	1	0	0	1	1	0	0	0	1
Manpur	1	1	1	1	1	0	0	0	1	1	1	1	1	0	0	0	1
Dalli Rajhara	1	0	1	1	0	1	1	0	0	1	0	1	1	1	0	0	0
Brazil																	
Carajás (old mines)	1	1	1	0	0	1	1	1	0	0	0	0	1	1	1	1	0
Carajás (S11D)	1	1	1	0	0	0	1	0	0	0	0	0	1	1	1	1	0
Minas-Rio	1	1	1	0	0	1	0	0	0	0	0	0	1	0	0	0	0
Apolo	0	1	1	0	0	1	1	0	0	0	1	1	1	0	0	1	0
Casa de Pedra	1	1	0	1	1	1	0	0	0	0	0	1	1	1	0	1	0
Mina Del Rey	1	1	1	0	1	0	1	0	0	0	1	1	1	0	1	1	0
Corumbá	1	1	1	1	0	0	1	1	0	0	0	0	0	0	0	0	0

56 *How to apply QCA?*

Table 3.3 Legend of abbreviations used in the QCA tables

Abbreviation	Definition
Strategies used by resistance	
a	Organizing and politicizing a mass social movement
b	Campaigning by heterodox, nonmodernist, anti-mining framing
c	Physically nonviolent protesting is noted
d	Networking with other resistance groups
e1	Embedding electoral politics, for example, via targeted voting of politicians opposing mining or allying with politicians seeking mine closure while retaining movement autonomy
e2	Embedding institutional politics, for example, by acquiring progressive state-actor-led investigations via advocacy, successfully demanding that regulatory institutions intervene to uphold the rule of law, occupying key institutions, or crafting new institutions while maintaining autonomy
e3	Embedding judicial politics that helps the resistance in litigation in court against the project while retaining autonomy
f	Participation in private politics initiatives of companies (CSR, etc.) where an agreement is reached
g1	Armed revolutionary resistance used
g2	Threat of resistance by arms is explicit but no violence takes place
Economic outcomes	
EO1	All mines (and/or all projects) discontinued
EO2	Some mines closed, expansion extension and volume significantly curtailed, and/or very major impact on extraction style (e.g., nonmechanized, worker-controlled mine)
EO3	Expansion decelerated
Political outcomes	
PO1	Transnational spread of resistance
PO2	National spread of political and economic outcomes from this locality
PO3	Locally enduring and strong resistance capacities and willingness created
PO4	Armed revolutionary agency created and spread across states by the conflict experience of the resistance

the roles of corporate agency and primary resource frontiers). In Carajás, the resistance faced Vale's plan to build S11D, a massive new mine, and the wishes of Vale, the government, and powerful third-party buyers to retain the Carajás mine, which is the world's largest iron ore mine and the greatest source of the company's profits. In Minas-Rio, the resistance faced a mining company called Anglo American, which has a multi-billion-dollar project with sunk costs amounting to billions. It is no wonder that the resistance there has "only" managed to slow down expansion. What these movements lacked in economic outcomes, they made up for in political advantage. In my first evaluation, the Minas-Rio resistance seemed to have managed to create locally (PO3) and nationally (PO2) important political outcomes in terms of resistance capacities, and the mobilization in Carajás was instrumental in creating a transnational (PO1) Vale resistance front.

In Corumbá, the fourth anomalous case where EO2 was not reached, the outcome can be explained by the use of private politics to end the conflict by agreement, thus weakening the willingness to resist. Movement demands channeled to the government via corporations are often more powerful than pleas directly from the movement. These demands, which came through corporate channels, have resulted in the liberation of a greater number of resources (material compensation) in a number of cases, including the MST exchanges with Vale in Carajás, Pará. However, such private politics are a dangerous path for mobilization as they are based on isolated local resistance, rather than a large and strong mass movement. The example of Corumbá, on the border of Mato Grosso do Sul with Bolivia, exemplifies the dangers of private politics. On the basis of my analysis of Diogo Rocho's notes on the Corumbá case, taken in April 2014 for the EJOLT Environmental Justice Atlas,[1] the reason the local indigenous peoples' and NGOs' joint resistance against the Corumbá iron ore mine expansion failed (though they used all strategies a–e) was that they mostly relied on strategy f, private negotiations with companies. Significantly, the movement did not even manage to decelerate the expansion or create a lasting mobilization, as it was satisfied with the promise of a new study on impacts funded by the companies. The market-led contraction of mining in Corumbá might have also impacted resistance willingness.[2]

Table 3.2 suggests that local strategies alone cannot explain the outcomes in all cases; one must study the contexts and other contingencies. In particular, corporate agency and its connection to government strategies must be considered to capture a fuller picture. This point notwithstanding, it is surprising how many cases are explained by Table 3.2. These cases are in the majority. In most of these cases, the use of strategies to build and exert resistance capacities has led to significant economic outcomes. This finding suggests that, as heuristic tools, strategies a–g are able to capture a large part of more general dynamics; by this I mean, strategies that are part of larger political dynamics and contingencies. These strategies are not analytical tools that are blind to contexts, they are dynamic concepts.

Table 3.4 summarizes the cases that led to economic outcome 1, the closure of all mines or projects (EO1). What were the commonalities between the strategies used in these cases? What were the alternative pathways?

On the basis of the QCA, abstention from the use of private politics ($f = 0$) was a causal condition in all cases where mining was discontinued.

58 How to apply QCA?

Table 3.4 Cases where all mines or projects were discontinued (before 2015)

Country	Cases	a	b	c	d	e1	e2	e3	f	g1	g2	EO1
India	Goa	1	1	1	1	0	1	1	0	0	0	1
	Kudremukh	1	1	1	1	0	0	1	0	0	1	1
	Bellary	0	1	1	1	0	1	1	0	0	0	1
	Salem	1	0	1	0	0	0	0	0	0	0	1
	Tiruvannamalai	1	1	1	1	0	0	1	0	0	1	1
	Keonjhar (Banspal, etc.)	1	1	1	0	1	0	0	0	0	1	1
	Khandadhar (Sundargarh)	1	1	1	1	1	1	1	0	0	0	1
	Rowghat	1	1	1	1	0	1	1	0	1	1	1
	Manpur	1	0	1	0	0	0	0	0	1	1	1
Brazil	Apolo	0	1	1	1	0	1	1	0	0	0	1
	Mina Del Rey	1	1	0	1	1	1	0	0	0	0	1

In addition, all cases except Salem and Manpur used some form of state embedding (e1–e3). I have removed Kawardha from the list as there was no active resistance against the iron ore project, which renders this case irrelevant for a consideration of resistance strategies' role. Salem could have been listed as having used e2, institutional politics, if demanding that a state institution produce a document could be considered state embedding (although this would be an overreach, as e1–e3 all refer to very active embedding and advocacy with the state with the goal of allying with some sector of the state and some powerholders or even becoming one; in Salem, the movement eschewed such state embedding). For an action to be included as a form of state embedding, the resistance must clearly partake in coproducing new, state-mediated politics (for example, the establishment of a new regulatory institution) or changing the existing rules (for example, through the creation of new, lasting ties between bureaucrats or judges and activists) (see Kröger 2020). In Manpur, EO1 seems to have been achieved primarily via armed revolutionary agency (g). Armed revolutionary resistance (g1), when used alone, seems to be sufficient to cause mine closures, while just the threat of using arms (g2), when used alone, requires the simultaneous use of peaceful resistance strategies to make a difference. Thus, armed revolutionary resistance (g1) is an alternative pathway, and the threat of using arms (g2) is not a necessary strategy to block investments.

Protest (c) was a necessary condition in all of the other cases that followed the nonarmed path of resistance except one, Mina Del Rey. However, in that case, the mass social movement resisting the mine, which even included the city's mayor and many other politicians, explicitly voiced its willingness to hit the streets at any time if needed. This threat, made to the Vale company and pro-mine authorities, appeared in the news and was very real. This comparison shows that protest is a necessary condition for movements that do not have a clear government ally, while those that do should nevertheless show the ability and willingness to protest.

How to use contradictory configurations?

The QCA truth table revealed that Mina Del Rey shared the same set of conditions as Casa de Pedra (same values for a–g), yet differed in relation to the EO1 outcome. These situations in QCA, where two or more studied sets produce a different outcome yet have identical configurations of conditions, are called contradictory configurations. QCA textbooks suggest that such cases should be used as valuable information for revisiting the data and the truth tables and one should try to resolve the issue by specifying the strategy, adding a new condition, or some other means (Rihoux and De Meur 2009). The final goal of QCA is typically to arrive at a more parsimonious explanation, a minimal formula, which is also the key goal of the Boolean logic used in QCA. However, the addition of more conditions or specifications might add more complexity and, thus, take one farther from the goal of finding a simple solution formula to a given puzzle.

The aforementioned contradictory configurations can be used as a basis for providing an explanation for when resistance does not have to opt for open protests. Later in this chapter, I will show how I explored 12 other contingency and contextual factors to explain the cases. These included three conditions wherein Casa de Pedra differed from Mina Del Rey; these three offered the possibility, through the means of adding new conditions, to specify what is important when explaining the outcomes of investment politics. These two cases had marked differences: In Mina Del Rey, the ore went primarily to China and the targeted company was large and used sophisticated countertactics against the resistance, while none of these conditions was active in the Casa de Pedra case. However, counterintuitively, the Mina Del Rey project was discontinued while Casa de Pedra was not. This suggests that the solution to the discrepancy lies elsewhere, beyond the conditions included in this QCA. As I will further discuss later, this difference can be explained by the fact that the resistance in Casa de Pedra did not even seek to shut down the old, existing mine. Therefore, at this point, one could add one more condition or delimit the set of cases by selecting only those cases where the resistance aimed to discontinue all mining or projects in the area and separating out the cases where the goal of the resistance was something less ambitious. To add this condition, I needed to get new information for each of the cases to evaluate whether the local resistance wanted to keep part of the existing mines or proposed projects running or to discontinue all mining ventures. However, this kind of information is difficult to attain for all of the cases, especially a posteriori. In these situations, the contradictory configuration can be explained verbally when reporting the research findings or in writing as I do here.

Contradictory configurations are spotted more easily by using the QCA Excel tool or other QCA tools available. These tools mark such configurations with the letter C. I recommend reflecting deeply on these contradictions, as they can be especially useful lessons for future research. For example, on the basis of the preceding contradiction and its analysis, I would recommend that future research on social movements should pay much closer attention, while collecting data in the field, to the key goals of the local population vis-à-vis the investment project that changes or purports to change their local environment. Are they campaigning for a ban on extractivist activities altogether? Or is the key goal to obtain more compensation for the locals, while the extraction per se is not such a problem? What goals do distinct resistance groups have in the same area, if the resistance is not clearly more or less united in its front and goals? In this, a serious definition of what counts as resistance needs to be undertaken. For example, steel plant trade unions that are advocating primarily for the nationalization of mineral deposits should not be counted as parts of the resistance to extractivism, because their goal is more related to the modality of mining and who is mining. In the case of Casa de Pedra, however, several mining specialists in the town joined the organized resistance group against the mine expansion in order to stall or discontinue it, so in this case there clearly was a visible and locally dominant resistance group.

On the basis of the lesson from this contradictory configuration, there needs to be more recognition in the field that there can be very distinct goals for different resistance groups in each locality, and even within the same locality. I would recommend that future research that uses QCA on topics similar to mine start by cataloguing a new condition for each of the resistance goals found. In my case, the goals I found included the following: To discontinue all operations; to change the style of extraction or to diminish its size; to obtain more compensation; to better regulate the industry, with less pollution; to create more jobs; or some other explicit, empirically backed goal that crops up in the open interviews and observations of meetings and rallies or in campaign materials of the resistance or other local groups wanting to have a say regarding an investment. After undertaking this initial step, one could run the QCA to see how these different goal conditions are related to different outcomes, that is, to what degree do movements attain the goals they are seeking. I have tried to do this by identifying three different economic outcome degrees and four different political outcomes, as all of these outcomes were present in the database and were voiced as goals by some proponents.

In this case, as is often the case in social sciences, the causes and outcomes are intricately linked and intermeshed. It is no wonder that the creation of armed resistance agency and capacity, as a political outcome, was related to the use of arms by resistance. What I wanted to emphasize with how I named this causal path was that it matters which path is initially taken with the resistance strategies, as these chosen paths tend to create a deepening spiral of that type of resistance agency, whether it be peaceful or violent. Furthermore, I wanted to see through the QCA analysis, which is made for this kind of comparison of multiple pathways, whether the simultaneous presence of other, peaceful strategies could hamper the creation of a deeper civil war context and revolutionary agency in the given locality.

After some rounds of testing which goals seem to be important and explaining the outcomes that one is most interested in, one can then proceed by focusing in more detail on those factors (e.g., resistance goals) by going back and forth between the conditions and the field. In my case, I followed this strategy and included the search for compensation by resistance into strategy f, which seeks to find a stakeholder compensation package and to deal directly with the company. Quite a few resistance groups to extractive projects do seek compensation, at least if they see that this is the most realistic option available. Yet, I was surprised to find that such cases are actually a minority, as this is contrary to the claims made by many scholars. In most cases, resistance was much fiercer and wanted to shut down extractivist operations. Because this surfaced as the key goal, I primarily focused on this outcome and did not specify the different resistance goals in more detail.. However, I would recommend adding one new condition to future truth tables on this issue, one that identifies two broad categories for the goal of resistance in a given case. One should denote whether the aim of the resistance was to discontinue the investments; the 0 QCA value would indicate that the goal was something other than this, something less radical and brave (e.g., compensation, change in style, more jobs).

In the setting of this new condition, I think it is also crucial to create distinct truth tables for distinct time periods, because resistance goals do tend to change as the conflicts and projects linger on. It is important to capture how possible changes in goals might affect the outcomes, either by weakening the desired goal or by making it stronger. One could also use temporal QCA to spot this possible change over time [see Ragin and Strand (2008) to learn more about temporal QCA]. However, in order to observe this temporal change, one would not only visit multiple field sites but visit them two or more times after a certain time lapse. This would mean much more field work, especially as one should strive to do one's own ethnographic observations to avoid the problem of different persons observing different things in the field. Yet, although it creates a very complex database, multi-sited, longitudinal ethnographic research could provide extremely valuable information and lead to major theoretical insights on social change around a given phenomenon. One would need to use some tool to organize the data and observations for systematic comparisons with such a large research project or set of projects. The production of different QCA tables and use of the tools of temporal QCA and incorporated comparisons would be extremely valuable in this task, as one can easily lose track of all the moving parts in such an analysis.

After these thoughts on what to do with contradictory configurations, I will move forward with reviewing the example tables to illustrate other points on how to practically apply QCA.

Identifying necessary key factors

Interestingly, Table 3.4 suggests that other resistance strategies—apart from protesting and restraining from private politics—do not necessarily have to be used for mining to be discontinued. For example, the creation of a mass social movement (strategy a) was not an active strategy in either the Bellary or the Apolo case. In Bellary, this strategy was tried, but a large part of the population was pro-mining and fearful of the "mining mafia" operating in the area (see Kröger 2020). Thus, a mass movement could not be created; instead, an NGO used institutional and judicial politics to close down the mine. While the NGO gathered some people for protests and campaigning, it did not do so in a way that would count as a local mass movement with thousands of active resistance members. In the case of Apolo, the NGO was very small at the beginning, but very professional, and as in Bellary, it performed most of the work that led to stalling the Vale project. Later, it turned into a social movement that may become a mass movement in the future, as the fate of the project has not been fully decided. A professional NGO can suffice instead of a mass movement, but this strategy may also backfire. In Bellary, a large part of the population now wants to reopen the mines, as they had not participated in producing the outcome. In the case of Apolo, the NGO successfully managed to turn itself into a movement and started to markedly change attitudes in its local area in Minas Gerais, a political outcome supporting the longevity of economic outcomes.

Campaigning (strategy b) is not necessary, as the case of Salem demonstrates. The resistance movement focused on swiftly organizing and politicizing a mass social movement, which marched to the authorities, occupied their building, and demanded to see the mine documents. After the documents were made available, they showed drastic irregularities and corruption, and the episode was over quickly. The campaign did not have to reach out to the hearts of the people in the larger audience as the case was already won. The Salem movement skipped campaigning and state embedding by going straight to protesting. This is an anomalous case because, typically, heterodox, normative campaigning is needed to raise the profile of the issue, not only for potential movement members but also for decision makers, the target, and third parties. In Salem, the mobilizing work was so effective and swift (physically going door to door around a relatively small hill) that the kind of mass audience, internet blogging conducted in Goa to spread alternative framings of mining over many years was not needed. I would suggest that leaving campaigning out can be a viable option in a small, tight, and typically (peri)urban case where it is possible for key activists to mobilize a crowd quickly.

Additionally, networking (strategy d), the creation of active networks between different resistance organizations from the same or another region, was not used by resistance groups in Salem or Keonjhar. However, it should be noted that, once its own victory was won, the Salem movement started helping others win their battles via networking. In Keonjhar, the movement operated alone under a single NGO. At one critical point in its story, when its key activists were detained under allegations of being Maoist guerrillas—this was not true—the movement received support and solidarity from human rights organizations and other NGOs based elsewhere. However, most of its outcomes had already been obtained beforehand, and these NGOs helped the movement liberate its activists and maintain the rule of law, but did not help perform their grassroots mobilizing work. Only later, after this episode, did the movement start to think about networking. Nonetheless, the movement mostly was not known to other movements in the same state who were resisting their "own" projects, and networking in general was just starting between different local resistance groups opposing iron ore mining expansion in Odisha. There were some intellectuals in the capital and elsewhere who were more knowledgeable about the situations in different parts of the state; however, such knowledge does not constitute networking without actions such as strategy-sharing meetings, joint protests, state embedding, or the replication of a successful strategy or resistance model.

This point notwithstanding, networking was helpful for most movements; Salem and Keonjhar are exceptions. Furthermore, in the latter case, the violent detention of movement members might have been prevented if the movement had been better networked before the incident, in which case the suspicions or allegations that it was a Maoist front organization would have been harder to sustain. A lone movement in a distant rural area is more open to suspicion than a local section of a large network with well-connected member organizations.

In the comparison of the relationship of state embedding (e1–e3) with mine closures, electoral politics (e1) were used in four cases, institutional politics (e2) in 11 cases, and judicial politics (e3) in 10 cases. These were all useful tools for the movements, but there are also dangers in using such tools, such as losing movement autonomy or losing the ability to use other strategies.

There are many other conclusions that can be drawn based on the findings in Table 3.2. For example, if we focus on PO2, the national spread of political and economic outcomes from a locality, as a dependent variable, then we find six cases, four in Brazil and two in India. They all shared the following strategies: Campaigning (b), embedding in institutional politics (e2), and abstaining from private politics (f = 0); armed revolutionary resistance was not used (g1 = 0). Notably, in these upstream struggles against extractivism wherein the local outcomes clearly traveled nationally and impacted the politics and economy of extractivism elsewhere, the movements actively engaged in democratizing and winning over the bureaucratic institutions of the state by direct engagement with them. The case of coproducing the Shah Commission in India allowed local movements to expand their role significantly, boost the reach of progressive state institutions, and thus spread the possibility of contention nationally.[3] These movements did not lose time or energy in engaging in private politics with companies; rather, they relied on state embedding.

The QCA tables should be used to cross-examine different factor and outcome combinations. When I examined the greenfield investments (seven cases), in all cases except two the resistance managed to block the investments (until 2015) from being realized (EO1).[4] This outcome suggests that it is easier to achieve drastic economic outcomes when resisting new projects. When I examined the brownfield cases, including the creation of new mines in an area that already had mines, all mining and projects were discontinued in less than half of the cases (6 out of 15). However, the cases that achieved the transnational spread of resistance (PO1) were cases of brownfield mining, which suggests that it is easier to mobilize and create global activist networks against established rather than projected mines. This political outcome of creating a new global resistance front might be more important in the long run than obtaining economic outcomes.

The necessary strategies for resistance aimed at blocking greenfield projects (and achieving this outcome) were protesting (c) and abstaining from private politics (f). However, alone these two strategies were not sufficient causal conditions. Rather, it was the use of a context-specific mix of supporting strategies, together with the necessary strategies, that led to the outcome. In the brownfield projects, the necessary condition to obtain mine closures included only abstention from private politics (f). However, if only the pathway of nonarmed resistance was considered, then campaigning (b) and some form of state embedding with autonomy (e) were also necessary strategies. If armed resistance was used, then these latter strategies were not necessary. Interestingly, if only the path of peaceful resistance was used, then the use of g2 (threat of resistance by arms made explicit by someone resisting, but without violence actually taking place) did not influence the outcome for better or worse from the resistance perspective. This finding suggests that the safest, most peaceful route that has the greatest influence on mining is for the resistance to use at least strategies b, c, and e, but not use f.

Sufficient resistance strategies causing drastic investment impacts

For the purpose of studying the outcomes obtained by the simultaneous use of all strategies a–e, which has been hypothesized to be sufficient to explain how and when resistance plays a key role in investment politics, I united the strategies—electoral (e1), institutional (e2), and judicial (e3) state embedding while retaining autonomy—into one causal condition called E (state embedding by a resistance group while retaining autonomy; the presence of any of the conditions e1–e3 was sufficient to be classified in this category). Table 3.5 shows the cases where the concatenation of a–e was used and the related outcomes. This type of QCA analysis can reveal sufficient causal condition complexes.

Table 3.5 shows that there were eight cases where the resistance used strategies a–e. Significantly, it seems that the context did not completely impede the ability to use all of a–e. For example, the civil war context of Rowghat, with simultaneous armed revolutionary resistance, did not impede the larger resistance movement from using all of a–e and, thus, most effectively boosting peaceful resistance. Furthermore, neither the case type (greenfield or brownfield) nor engagement with private politics (f = 1) influenced the possibility of using the full spectrum of strategies a–e. The interesting anomalies in the use of strategy f are Corumbá and Carajás. However, the use of f in Carajás coincided with the movement retaining its autonomy. MST has an especially strong, organizing strategy that ensured autonomy in multiple senses of the term. The resistance in Carajás did not achieve EO1 or EO2 while most other cases where all of a–e were used did, suggesting that the use of f would have mitigated the impact of using a–e. The three cases without EO1 or EO2 are all in Brazil, suggesting a contrast with India. Since 2000, in the Indian political system the resistance against iron ore mining, when using all strategies a–e, has managed to dramatically influence investment outcomes, blocking all projects and closing down existing mines. This included all of the states studied, those with civil war contexts and those with non–civil war contexts.

Table 3.5 Peaceful resistance by the concatenated use of all strategies a-e

Country	Cases	a	b	c	d	E	f	g1	g2	EO1	EO2	EO3	PO1	PO2	PO3	PO4	Case type
India	Goa	1	1	1	1	1	0	0	0	1	1	1	0	1	1	0	1
	Kudremukh	1	1	1	1	1	0	0	0	1	1	1	0	0	1	0	1
	Tiruvannamalai	1	1	1	1	1	0	0	1	1	1	1	0	0	1	0	0
	Khandadhar (Sundargarh)	1	1	1	1	1	0	0	0	1	1	1	0	0	1	0	0
	Rowghat	1	1	1	1	1	0	1	1	1	1	1	0	0	1	0	0
Brazil	Carajás (old)	1	1	1	1	1	1	0	0	0	0	0	1	1	1	1	1
	Minas-Rio	1	1	1	1	1	0	0	0	0	0	1	0	1	1	0	0
	Corumbá	1	1	1	1	1	1	0	0	0	0	0	0	0	0	0	0

This is a major finding. The causal relation of using the five key strategies (a–e) with iron ore mining politics in India is drastic, as this was the ultimate (but not necessarily the proximate) cause for discontinuations. This finding corroborates the hypothesis for India, but not for Brazil. Further highlighting the difference between Brazil and India, I found that there were also cases in India where not all of the strategies (a–e) were used, yet there were mine closures and/or blockages. This finding suggests that a lesser array of strategies can also lead to drastic economic outcomes in some contexts. This discrepancy (and the contingencies studied later) suggests that the context, corporate agency, and target of mobilization are more difficult in Brazil than in India and require a fuller use of different, complementary, and concatenated resistance strategies.

As a generalizable conclusion, the sufficient condition for mining or project discontinuation in India was the use of all peaceful resistance strategies a–e. This finding means that not all of the strategies (a–e) were necessary in every case, although prescience would be required to know which of them could be safely overlooked. A consistent finding that I observed was the surprise that activists felt when they learned that they had not known the context well enough and that they had not been able to foresee, predict, or assess opportunities correctly. In plain terms, it seems that resistance movements have a better chance of success when they use a larger array of resistance strategies.

The impact of armed revolutionary agency on mining expansion

In addition to peaceful contention, the other major pathway for drastically influencing investments is armed revolutionary resistance. Table 3.6 summarizes these cases, providing an overview of the outcomes and how the use of this pathway relates to peaceful resistance.

Table 3.6 suggests that armed revolutionary resistance (g1 = 1) was causally related to at least the major political outcome of armed revolutionary agency created and spread across states by the conflict experience of the resistance (PO4), as well as major economic outcomes (EO2) in all cases and project stalling or mine closure (EO1) in two cases. However, while it is understandable that g1 feeds into a further spread of armed resistance agency elsewhere (PO4), g1 was not the only possible explanatory factor for the economic outcomes (EO1 and EO2) in Table 3.6. Unsurprisingly, the political outcome deepened and spread armed revolutionary agency (PO4); yet, even more interestingly, these cases also experienced the creation of locally enduring and strong resistance capacities and willingness (PO3). However, larger resistance, nationally or globally, was not forged or spread by these experiences; thus, these seem to be separate causal paths with

68 How to apply QCA?

Table 3.6 Armed revolutionary agency and resistance outcomes

Country	Cases	Strategies									Outcomes							Case type
		a	b	c	d	E	f	g1	g2	EO1	EO2	EO3	PO1	PO2	PO3	PO4	
India	West Singhbhum	1	1	1	1	0	0	0	1	0	1	1	0	0	1	1	1
	Dantewada	1	1	0	1	0	0	1	1	0	1	1	0	0	1	1	1
	Rowghat	1	1	1	1	0	0	1	1	1	1	1	1	0	1	1	0
	Manpur	1	0	1	0	0	0	1	1	1	1	1	0	0	1	1	1

How to apply QCA? 69

differing political outcomes. The Maoists did not use strategy E; however, the peaceful resistance separate from the Maoist groups and active resistance in the same cases used E in some cases. For example, in Dantewada, outsiders used the courts to try to indirectly decelerate the negative impacts of mining via petitioning to outlaw paramilitaries, while in Rowghat, nonarmed activists embedded state institutions (e2) to demand the rule of law and that the constitutional land rights for Adivasis be upheld.

The tables summarize the actions of not only one social actor against a single mine but also all the actors in the area typically resisting many investments—this makes more sense, as their impacts are pooled. Table 3.6 does not make it possible to claim that armed revolutionary agency alone could lead to the desired economic outcomes. In fact, many of my informants said that in many places, the Maoists do not even seek to close down all mines, a goal more typical of nonarmed resistance.[5] The use of a–c in the major armed conflict areas brings many other benefits for overall resistance. The use of these three strategies (a–c) builds and/or sustains a large, local, peaceful resistance that targets extractivism, ensuring that armed resistance is critical of irresponsible investments. In the absence of such peaceful contention against extractivism and in the presence of a more extractivist and self-determinist agency, such as in India's Northeast (see Karlsson 2011), armed resistance has not been critical of mining or revolutionary. The armed resistance in parts of Chhattisgarh and Jharkhand builds on a strong general willingness to resist extractivism among local Adivasis, for whom a long trajectory of such resistance against outsiders is incorporated into their tribal identities and modes of organization.

The QCA tables provide an overview of complex causal conditions, where the studied causes used together might lead to outcomes. Thus, in this analysis, it can be supposed that the reason why armed resistance was effective was that in all cases the overall resistance in the same areas also used at least the key peaceful mobilization strategies a and c. In many cases they were using b and d as well. However, it should be noted that I documented only those instances where I had proof—Manpur and Dantewada might have had a fuller use of a–d if examined more closely—but I could not visit these areas due to the armed conflict and had to rely on in-depth interviews and existing data and research.

The csQCA truth table analysis for Table 3.6 to find out the implicants (causal condition configurations) and solutions for economic outcome 1 (EO1) revealed two: The cases of Manpur and Rowghat, which both reached project discontinuations during the period studied. These cases shared the use of strategies a, c, g1, and g2 and while not using f, which suggested that these five are necessary causal conditions to reach the most impressive economic outcomes in a civil war situation. That is, besides using and threatening to use arms, resistance in such contexts should also organize mass social movements, protest peacefully, and avoid private politics because—on the basis of these data—mere armed resistance was not enough.

QCA of complex contextual factors and contingencies

To test the hypothesis that was corroborated by the preceding analysis for India and for many (but not all) of the Brazilian cases, I next studied the role of several alternative, competing, and complementary explanatory factors. This analysis was also important in defining the extent to which strategies a–g are important to explain the overall investment politics and to rule out factors that do not seem to be particularly relevant. The contingencies that I could place into Boolean logic are summarized in Table 3.7. The systematic comparison of these contingencies reveals the ways in which the political context, geography, economic sector, greater mobilization trajectory, variation in corporate agency and third parties, and other dynamics of contention, such as ethnic relations in the investment area, may influence the outcomes of investment politics in conjunction with resistance efforts. Table 3.7 includes 12 conditions that were divided into subsections to explore how a set of competing and complementary factors might be causally related to different outcomes. Table 3.7 is not yet a truth table, but specific truth tables can be created from this table to test for the capacity of different explanations to reveal, complement, or challenge the findings thus far. I also use QCA here, in the contingency section, to explore the validity of the claim that strategies a–g matter.

Table 3.8 should be used in conjunction with Table 3.7 as it is a legend for the abbreviations used in Table 3.7

The logic for selecting each of these factors was discussed at length in the prior chapters of this book, and such explanations need to be given to offer transparency to the causal condition and outcome selection in QCA. The possible hypothesized relations and causes (sufficient and necessary) for each factor should also be discussed. I explained that, on the basis of my prior studies, I hypothesized that strategies a–e, when used together, are both sufficient and necessary for explaining when there is a notable slowing down or discontinuation of investment projects. I set out degrees for assessing the impact by establishing different dependent variables, for example, when all mining was discontinued (EO1).

A truth table analysis of all the causal conditions in Table 3.7 and their relation to EO1 reveals that each case has different contextual and contingency settings, because no clear, minimal formula emerges that could explain the outcome across more than one case. The purpose here is not

Table 3.7 Contextual factors and contingencies in Indian and Brazilian iron mining politics

Cases	Contingencies												Outcomes								
	a1	a2	a3	P1	P2	P3	T1	T2	GE1	CD1	CD2	CD3	EO1	EO2	EO3	PO1	PO2	PO3	PO4
India																			
Goa	1	1	1	0	0	0	1	1	0	1	1	0	1	1	1	0	1	1	0
Kudremukh	1	1	1	1	0	0	1	0	0	1	0	0	1	1	1	0	0	0	0
Bellary	0	1	0	0	0	0	0	1	1	1	1	0	1	1	1	0	1	0	0
Salem	1	1	0	0	0	0	1	0	0	1	1	0	1	1	1	0	1	1	0
Tiruvannamalai	1	0	1	0	0	1	0	0	0	1	0	0	1	1	1	0	0	0	0
Joda	0	0	0	0	1	0	0	1	1	1	1	0	0	1	1	0	0	0	0
Keonjhar (Banspal, etc.)	1	0	0	0	0	0	0	0	1	0	1	0	1	1	1	0	0	0	0
Khandadhar (Sundargarh)	0	0	1	0	1	0	0	0	1	1	0	0	1	1	1	0	0	0	0
Pre-2005 Sundargarh	0	0	0	0	0	0	0	0	1	1	1	1	1	1	1	0	0	0	0
Post-2005 Sundargarh	0	0	0	0	0	0	0	0	1	1	1	1	1	1	1	0	0	0	0
West Singhbhum	0	0	1	1	0	0	0	1	1	0	1	1	0	1	1	0	1	1	1
Dantewada	0	0	0	1	0	0	0	1	1	0	1	1	0	1	1	1	0	0	1
Rowghat	0	0	0	1	0	0	0	1	1	0	1	1	0	1	1	1	0	0	1
Manpur	0	0	0	0	0	0	0	1	1	0	0	0	0	1	1	1	0	1	1
Dalli Rajhara	1	0	1	1	1	0	0	1	1	0	1	0	0	1	1	0	0	0	1
Kawardha	0	0	0	0	0	0	0	0	1	1	1	0	n/a	n/a	n/a	n/a	n/a	n/a	n/a
Brazil																			
Carajás	0	0	0	1	1	0	1	1	1	0	1	1	0	0	1	1	1	1	0
S11D	0	0	0	1	1	0	1	1	1	0	0	0	0	0	1	0	0	1	0
Minas-Rio	0	0	0	0	1	0	1	1	1	1	0	0	1	1	1	0	1	1	0
Apolo	1	1	0	1	0	0	0	0	1	1	0	0	1	1	0	0	0	0	0
Casa de Pedra	1	1	0	0	0	1	1	1	0	1	0	1	0	1	1	0	1	1	0
Mina Del Rey	1	1	0	0	0	1	1	1	0	1	0	1	1	1	1	0	1	1	0
Corumbá	0	0	0	0	0	0	0	0	0	0	1	0	0	0	0	0	0	0	0

Table 3.8 Legend for the contingencies in Indian and Brazilian mining politics

Abbreviation	Definition
Specificities in the context of resistance organization	
a1	Local middle classes largely supported resistance
a2	Key resistance group included urban, middle-class professionals in key positions
a3	Several cross-class, interethnic, or intersector resistance groups
Political role and type of targets	
P1	Primarily central-government-led expansion
P2	A primary national resource frontier
P3	A deep ethnic injustice: Mining that represents a profound ethnic injustice by mostly benefiting elite ethnic groups and perpetrating forestland loss that mostly affects vulnerable communities (e.g., indigenous groups)
Third-party roles	
T1	Tourism, agriculture, or other significant mining-critical industries present
T2	Ore went or would go primarily to China
Geographic factors	
GE1	High-quality ore (over 60% average iron content)
Corporate agency differences	
CD1	Underestimation of the resistance potential by the targets
CD2	Size of the company(ies): 1 = large, 0 = small
CD3	Sophisticated corporate countertactics to curb mobilization

to try to find a very broad generalization but to provide space for the individual characteristics of each case and use this information to challenge the claims of earlier generalizations about the roles of conditions a–g. This truth table exercise helps to more systematically identify and more explicitly lay out which factors emerged as important based on multi-sited ethnography and prior scholarship. I am more interested in determining how many cases followed a certain pattern or set of conditions or produced a similar outcome. I want to identify sets of cases that seem to function similarly. This makes more sense in multi-sited ethnography, as there can be major contextual differences across which the policy-making politics work differently, through at least somewhat distinct dynamics, mechanisms, strategies, and actors.

csQCA of all Table 3.7 conditions (12) in relation to EO1 reveals several subgroups of implicants. For example, Corumbá, Minas-Rio, Joda, pre-2005 Sundargarh, post-2005 Sundargarh, and S11D are all cases where mining or projects were not discontinued. The QCA Excel tool helps to quickly identify the conditions shared among these, which are the absence of middle-class support (a1) and the absence of an assorted group of ethnically, sectorially, and/or class-differentiated resistance groups (a3), but the presence of a large company as the miner (CD2). This information is useful for several reasons as it suggests that middle-class support might be important, as well as the presence of many different resistance groups, and that large companies are harder to resist. This allows for contextualizing why strategies a–g might work differently in distinct contextual dynamics.

When QCA was used for Table 3.7, many other reasons also surfaced for the group of cases where EO1 was not achieved, which gave contextual explanations for the outcome. For example, there were six cases (Corumbá, Post-2005 Sundargarh, S11D, West Singhbhum, Carajás, Dalli Rajhara) where EO1 was not the outcome. The two conditions that this set of cases shared were the absence of urban professionals as key activists (a2) and the use of sophisticated countertactics by the corporations (CD3). This brings to the table some important additions. In social movement research, one should not focus merely on the movements but also look at what other locals do and what the targets do, in this case urban professionals and corporations, respectively. These actions by potentially powerful, yet not always active would-be resistance actors and corporations, help to further explain why the preceding six cases did not present discontinuation of all mining operations, even though in several of these cases the resistance used many of the key strategies a–e. Yet, the main finding of a QCA based on Table 3.7 is that these contextual and contingency factors, as subsets or together, cannot explain the cases and their outcomes as well as the key resistance strategies studied in prior tables. This serves to support the hypothesis on the centrality of the five key resistance strategies.

Let us consider the role of the factors in Table 3.7 in relation to the outcomes of the cases by starting with the first set of strategies, a1–a3. There is a striking discrepancy between economic and political outcomes when the middle classes largely support resistance (a1). Almost all of these cases (nine in total) corresponded to mine closure or blockage (EO1), and in the two cases where this did not happen (Dalli Rajhara and Casa de Pedra) the economic outcome was a very important change in extraction style and a remarkable deceleration. In fact, these were the goals of these movements, which signifies that, in all cases with a1, the resistance achieved the economic outcome that it pursued. In contrast, only one case corresponded to the creation of global resistance (PO1) (Mina Del Rey), and the national spread of the political and economic curbing of extractivism (PO2) was achieved only in that same upstream struggle case and in Goa. This finding suggests that the support of the local middle class can help movements to achieve extremely impressive economic outcomes, but possibly at the cost of building global resistance (PO1), influencing the politics and economy of extractivism more nationally (PO2), or boosting armed revolutionary agency (PO4). Thus, middle-class support may offer a shortcut to busting extractivist booms, but not to the boosting of resistance agency. The support of the local middle class can also be useful for avoiding civil war.

The presence of urban professionals as key activists (a2, seven cases) typically correlated with middle-class support. The only case where this did not hold true was Bellary. However, middle-class support (a1) does not necessarily mean that the middle classes will lead the resistance, as in three out of the nine instances this was not the case.

Simultaneous pressure placed on expansion by an assorted group of ethnically, sectorially, and/or class-differentiated resistance groups (a3, 11 cases) was related to EO2 in all cases except one (old Carajás) and to EO1 in six cases. This suggests that a broader, compartmentalized spread of resistance can be quite important for obtaining the desired economic outcomes, although not as clearly as with a1. Given that three of the five non-EO1-corresponding cases were armed conflicts, this finding suggests that the splintering of resistance (a3) does not impede obtaining the desired outcomes (as some might expect) but typically supports favorable results, particularly in the most peaceful contexts.

In regard to the political roles and types of targets, when the area in question is represented by a primarily central-government-led mining expansion (P1, eight cases), meaning a very strong level of government support, mine closure or blockage occurred in three cases (Rowghat, Kudremukh, and Khandadhar, not considering Kawardha). The resistance in these three EO1 cases was well-built (using strategies a–e and even explicitly hinting that it could use arms in two of the cases). Outside Carajás, all cases with a strong governmental push had major economic victories for resistance and achieved at least EO2. These causal condition complexes suggest that a central government role (P1) is not a sufficient, necessary, or even an important contingency that explains resistance outcomes.

Primary national resource frontiers (P2, eight cases) showed much more armed revolutionary resistance (g1, three cases) than cases not having P2. Interestingly, P2 did not impede movements from achieving any of the economic or political outcomes, as all outcomes were achieved in the group of P2 cases. Resource frontiers do not define their political outcomes, which are borne by larger politics aside from extractivist expansion.

Mining that represents a profound ethnic injustice by mostly benefiting elite ethnic groups and by perpetuating forestland loss that mostly affects vulnerable communities (P3) was present in 14 cases, including 11 in India. All political and economic outcomes except global resistance (one case) were achieved in at least three cases, suggesting that P3 is not a necessary causal condition nor does it provide a sufficient explanation of investment or resistance outcomes. Notably, however, P3 coincided with the almost complete presence of mass social movements (a) and protests (c); both were present in all cases except Joda and post-2005 Sundargarh. Interestingly, the use of other strategies (b, d, e, and g) showed much greater variance. This finding suggests that people facing the condition of P3 most typically do and/or must resort to radical means, as they face constraints due to ethnic discrimination and/or ethnicity-based movement building in embedding the state or networking with other groups.

The role of third parties, such as tourism, agriculture, or any other significant industry whose members become critical of mining (T1), was present in only six cases, as shown in Table 3.9. For example, the textile industry owners in Salem became critical of the proposed mining expansion, which would have caused dust from the mining operations to ruin their textile mills as they were next to the proposed mining site. There was also an important tourism industry operating in places such as Goa and Tiruvannamalai, whose entrepreneurs were wary of potential or increasing damages to water quality and the environment, a contextual feature that could be seen as potentially helping the resistance. Thus, I compared whether this was the case or not.

Table 3.9 suggests that the presence of local industries whose members are critical of mining (which may be passive in their agency), while possibly playing a considerable role in many cases, was not a necessary or sufficient condition for explaining the outcomes. It is noteworthy that none of the six T1 cases was in an armed conflict area; rather, they were all in comparatively higher welfare regions of the countries (Goa, Karnataka, Tamil Nadu, and Minas Gerais). Industries critical of mining seemed to aid in achieving economic outcomes (EO1 obtained in five cases) but not particularly in fostering global or national coalitions (PO1, one case; PO2, two cases). Nonetheless, a significant alternative industry critical of mining may be an efficient condition for avoiding the creation of g1 (armed revolutionary resistance) and PO4 (armed revolutionary agency) (not present in any of these cases). Finally, industries critical of mining might allow the resistance to discard the use of arms in favor of one of the other strategies b–d. They are also unlikely to succumb to private politics with the miners (no cases with f).

China's role as buyer in the conflicts as a significant third party was considerable as T2 (ore went or would go primarily to China) was present in eight cases. Of the third parties, China was the most important. Significantly, of the eight cases of T2, only two were in India (Goa, Bellary) and the rest were in Brazil. This finding allowed me to deploy the element of international relations when I studied whether the different diplomatic and trade ties of Brazil and India with China influenced their domestic mining

Table 3.9 The role of third parties

Cases		a1	a2	a3	P1	P2	P3	T1	T2	GE1	CD1	CD2	a	b	c	d	e1	e2	e3	f	g1	g2	EO1	EO2	EO3	PO1	PO2	PO3	PO4	Case types
		\multicolumn{11}{c	}{Contingencies}	\multicolumn{10}{c	}{Strategies}	\multicolumn{7}{c	}{Outcomes}	
India	Goa	1	1	1	0	0	1	1	1	0	1	1	1	1	1	1	0	1	0	0	0	0	1	1	1	0	1	0	0	1
	Kudremukh	1	1	1	1	0	0	1	0	0	0	0	1	1	1	1	0	0	0	0	1	1	1	1	1	0	0	1	0	1
	Salem	1	1	0	0	0	0	1	0	0	0	1	1	0	1	0	0	0	0	0	0	0	1	1	1	0	0	0	0	0
	Tiruvannamalai	1	0	1	0	0	1	0	0	1	1	1	1	1	1	1	0	1	0	0	0	0	1	1	1	0	0	0	0	0
Brazil	Casa de Pedra	1	1	1	0	0	0	0	1	0	1	0	1	1	0	1	1	1	1	0	0	0	1	1	1	0	0	1	0	1
	Mina Del Rey	1	1	1	0	0	0	0	1	0	1	1	1	1	0	1	1	1	1	0	0	0	1	1	1	0	0	0	0	1

politics, policies, conflicts, socioenvironmental consequences, and investment outcomes. Interestingly, Chinese actors were not significant ore buyers in any of the contexts exhibiting armed revolutionary resistance (g1) or even potential armed conflict (g2) (zero cases out of the eight with T2). A growing number of studies concerning the global resource rush have examined China's role; the first wave of scholarship overemphasizes it, and the second looks for differences in how the Chinese resource rush might vary from the actions of the Global North (Edelman, Oya, and Borras 2013). My data allow examination of the extent to which different varieties of capitalism can be resisted or mobilized against and the kind of dynamics of contention and corporate-local and state-local population relations that Chinese "South-South relations" entail [or the relations of other BRICS (Brazil, Russia, India, China, South Africa) countries]. My analysis suggests that the Chinese third-party role can be used quite effectively in campaigning (strategy b, present in all cases) and did not impede important, economic outcomes sought by resistance (mine blockage or closure in four cases) or political outcomes from being achieved (global coalitions forged in three cases, national resistance spread in six cases, armed revolutionary agency in zero cases). This finding suggests that Chinese capital might be easier to resist (to govern) than capital from the traditional extractivist powers of the West, multinationals, or Indian and Brazilian national corporations and states.

Furthermore, I considered many geographic factors. Of these, I studied high-quality ore (over 60% iron content, GE1) via Boolean logic; thus, it was left as a factor for consideration after repeated rounds of removing unimportant or imprecise conditions. I found that 18 of the cases had high-quality iron ore. The quality of the ore might be expected to influence the dynamics of contention and corporate willingness to hang on to a resource site despite resistance, because high-quality iron ore is not found everywhere and is a very strategic resource. Five cases did not have high-quality ore in significant amounts (Goa, Kudremukh, Salem, Tiruvannamalai, and Corumbá). In the first four of these latter cases, resistance led to closures or blockages, which suggests that it may be easier, or more likely, to obtain significant economic outcomes when the targeted geography is not as rich in endowments.[6] This point notwithstanding, 12 of the 18 cases with high-quality ore also corresponded to mine closures or blockages, suggesting that endowments may be overcome by politics. My research on endowments and other geographic factors supports and deepens the research by Watts (2004) and Nugent and Robinson (2010), who problematize the notion of the "resource curse" and other straightforward claims that place primary explanatory importance on materiality to explain politics or the economy. Resources do not "produce" curses, but the vile (partly local) political dynamics do. This is not to deny that each commodity does not have its particularities in regard to politics. Materiality enables, but does not drive, extraction or its contraction, as sociopolitical processes either activate or inactivate the political potentialities in resources. My temporal data show that as resistance experience in iron ore projects accumulates, increasingly large numbers of iron projects are already being criticized in the preventive stage.

Finally, there are several ways that corporate agency may influence outcomes. The underestimation of the resistance potential by the targets (CD1) was present in eight cases. As Table 3.10 portrays, seven of these cases had EO1 (and in Casa de Pedra, EO1 was not even the goal of the resistance as the movement wanted to keep the old part of the mine open). Table 3.10 strongly supports the claim that when corporate agency underestimates the resistance potential, mobilization can have enormous impacts.

The strong presence of EO1 in the CD1 cases means that it became harder to suggest that the resistance could have achieved EO1 if not for corporate weaknesses. This conclusion supported the theoretical claim that movement analysis needs to be dynamic (McAdam, Tarrow, and Tilly 2001, 2008) and needs to include corporate agency to allow a broad understanding of how outcomes are determined. The database showed that resistance that faced corporate inattention or arrogance, in the form of CD1, could drop the use of one of the strategies a–e to obtain EO1. Additionally, it did not need to pursue its agenda through the use of private or armed politics. This point notwithstanding, the outcomes could not have been achieved with the sole presence of resistance underestimation. The presence of this causal condition seemed to ease the work of resistance, thus requiring relatively less effort to obtain greater economic (but not political) outcomes. Furthermore, because the struggle was not as difficult as in those cases where

Table 3.10 Underestimation of resistance potential by the targets (CD1)

Country	Cases	Strategies									Contingencies			Outcomes
		a	b	c	d	e1	e2	e3	f	g1	CD1	CD2	CD3	EO1
India	Goa	1	1	1	1	0	1	1	0	0	1	1	0	1
	Kudremukh	1	1	1	1	0	0	1	0	0	1	0	0	1
	Bellary	0	1	1	1	0	1	1	0	0	1	0	0	1
	Salem	1	0	1	0	0	0	0	0	0	1	1	0	1
	Tiruvannamalai	1	1	1	1	0	0	1	0	0	1	1	0	1
Brazil	Apolo	0	1	1	1	0	1	1	0	0	1	1	1	1
	Casa de Pedra	1	1	0	1	1	1	0	0	0	1	0	0	0
	Mina Del Rey	1	1	0	1	1	1	0	0	0	1	1	1	1

Table 3.11 Resistance targeting smaller companies (CD2 = 0)

Country	Cases	Strategies			Contingencies									Outcome
		a1	a2	a3	P1	P2	P3	T1	T2	GE1	CD1	CD2	CD3	EO1
India	Kudremukh	1	1	1	1	0	0	1	0	0	1	0	0	1
	Bellary	0	1	0	0	0	0	0	1	1	1	0	0	1
	Manpur	0	0	0	0	0	1	0	0	1	0	0	0	1
	Casa de Pedra	1	1	1	0	0	0	1	0	1	1	0	0	0

corporations expect resistance, however, the resistance created might not be particularly radical or strong.

The observation of the size of the company(ies) in the investment area (CD2) shows that the companies were relatively large in 19 cases and small in four cases. As shown in Table 3.11, the resistance targeting smaller companies (CD2 = 0) obtained EO1 in three cases (Casa de Pedra, where the resistance was not seeking EO1, was the fourth). This finding suggests that it might be easier to target smaller companies than to target larger companies. However, company size is by no means a necessary or sufficient condition for explaining outcomes.

Table 3.11 suggests that small companies did not use sophisticated corporate countertactics to curb mobilization (CD3), a corporate agency factor that relates to company size. In fact, the comparison between Table 3.11 and Table 3.12, which shows all the cases where CD3 was used, suggests that corporate countertactics provide a better explanation for economic outcomes than company size (if all other causal conditions are isolated), as resistance led to mine closures or blockages in only two of the eight cases with sophisticated corporate countertactics. Furthermore, in both Apolo and Mina Del Rey (Vale projects) while resistance was ongoing, Vale decided to focus on its iron ore operations in the Carajás region—this is another corporate agency factor that can strongly influence investment outcomes. Company size and corporate countertactics help to put the discussion of social movements into a larger context and to show how civil society resistance is often just one player in explaining resource booms, when mines are opened, and when companies change the locations of their mines.

However, my analysis demonstrates that, in resource busts, resistance can play a key role. In several cases where expansion was curbed in a major (EO2) or minor (EO3) way, the outcomes were achieved despite corporate tactics to counter resistance (CD3). This finding suggests that corporate agency is not necessary or sufficient to explain when resistance succeeds. Nonetheless, corporate countertactics seem to be a very important causal condition to consider. Two-thirds of the cases of resistance that achieved

80 *How to apply QCA?*

Table 3.12 Corporate countertactics to curb mobilization (CD3)

Country	Cases	Strategies			Contingencies										Outcomes				
		a1	a2	a3	P1	P2	P3	T1	T2	GE1	CD1	CD2	CD3	EO1	EO2	PO1	PO2	PO3
India	Post-2005 Sundargarh	0	0	0	0	1	1	0	0	1	0	1	1	0	1	0	0	0
	West Singhbhum	0	0	1	1	1	1	0	0	1	0	1	1	0	1	0	0	1
	Dalli Rajhara	1	0	1	0	0	0	0	0	1	0	1	1	0	1	0	0	1
Brazil	Carajás	0	0	1	1	1	1	0	1	1	0	1	1	0	0	1	1	1
	S11D	0	0	0	1	0	0	0	1	1	0	1	1	0	0	1	1	1
	Apolo	1	1	0	0	0	0	1	1	1	1	1	1	1	1	0	0	1
	Mina Del Rey	1	1	1	0	0	0	0	1	1	1	1	1	1	1	0	1	1
	Corumbá	0	0	0	0	0	1	0	1	0	0	1	1	0	0	0	0	0

How to apply QCA? 81

mine closures did not have to face CD3, while only one-fourth of the resistance cases that faced CD3 led to projects being blocked. Furthermore, these two cases (Apolo and Mina Del Rey) can be explained in part by other corporate strategies, which illustrates the importance of studying the side that is further pushing extractivism.

These findings concerning corporate agency suggest that it is important to study the role of CSR and other corporate strategies to explain investment, mining, and environmental politics, especially in cases with complex state-corporate-social movement conflicts. Next, I will utilize the preceding tables to show how one can use the raw format data tables to produce truth tables for the purpose of trying to find a minimal formula that is a more parsimonious explanation.

QCA minimal formula exercise

Normally, the key goal of QCA is to find a minimal formula, a short and clear explanation of the key causalities behind the outcome that interests one the most. In the project under scrutiny in this book, I was most interested in explaining when resources are left in the ground, that is, when an extractivist project is cancelled or discontinued for a longer period of time (EO1). I already identified that the two necessary strategies or causal conditions for this outcome to be reached are protesting and not engaging in stakeholder dialogues. Thus, at this point I dropped the other eight strategies from the set of ten strategies that I initially compared. I retained the outcome and strategies c and f for closer inspection in an effort to find a minimal formula that will explain the strategies by which the resistance is most likely to attain success in discontinuing extractivist operations.

QCA guidebooks suggest that it is best to focus on four to seven conditions and one outcome when trying to find a minimal formula (Rihoux and De Meur 2009). However, before reaching this stage, one typically must have gone through a much broader set of conditions to test them, as I have described previously. This was done not only for the purpose of finding the minimal formula but also because much important ethnographic and contextually meaningful data are lost in the process of delimiting the focus to four to seven conditions. In this sense, the previous analysis differs from most QCA studies, both in testing the limits of existing conventions in QCA and in offering new possibilities on how to combine a probabilistic dimension to exploring differences through QCA-based systematic comparison of complex data sets.

For the sake of transparency, one must always give an explanation when adding or removing conditions in QCA. It is important to discuss what was added and removed and why those decisions were made. Thus, as mentioned previously, I will now remove eight of the ten initial strategy conditions, as only two out of ten were found to be necessary causal conditions. Furthermore, the conditions of movement-building, campaigning, networking, state coproduction while retaining autonomy, and using arms or threatening to use them were partially added as these can either highlight particular nuances of the key strategies or explain distinct, context-influenced resistance paths. These are unlike the conditions of protesting and avoiding talks with corporations, which can be seen as more fundamental strategy choices across all types of contexts. Factor a served to highlight that NGOs, not just social movements, can successfully resist. Campaigning by nonmodernist framing highlighted the importance of running campaigns, especially in a way that challenges the monetization and commensurability claims of natural resource exploiters. Networking was emphasized to show how this can help movements that are isolated. State coproduction and embedding via electoral, institutional, or judicial means, while retaining autonomy, explored how movements can and should engage with the state instead of being anarchic and illustrated specific ways these actions have molded the state. All of these strategies were founded directly on empirical research and prior study of social movement studies and other relevant literatures. That is, these strategies were developed by both deduction and induction. Last, resistance by arms and the threat of their use were important factors to explain how resistance takes place in armed conflict contexts in India. Having completed the preceding analytical exercise on the meanings of these conditions, which yielded information about many things, I will next explore what configurations a QCA exercise toward parsimony yields.

Table 3.13 follows, which shows the impact of c and f on EO1. I produced this table with the aid of the Excel QCA tool, which allows one to easily select the conditions of interest for a truth table from the broader QCA table that contains all of the conditions and outcomes. I have removed the case of Casa de Pedra from the list of cases because the goal of the resistance was not to shut down all mining. I have also removed pre-2005 Sundargarh from the list because it was added to include a temporal element in the preceding analysis, as the dynamics in Sundargarh differed before 2005. For example, prior to 2005 there was protesting, but not after. Another reason for dropping the case of pre-2005 Sundargarh, which does result in contradictory configurations with some other cases, is because it is from a different time period. For the purpose of determining a minimal formula, if the reasons are clearly laid out, it is acceptable to carry out these simplifying exercises. After removing these cases, I ran the QCA Excel tool again, as it is best to do the removals one at a time and see how the solutions differ with each new iteration. This iteration did not produce meaningful solutions. For this reason, I dropped all of the cases in Brazil because protesting

Table 3.13 QCA truth table on necessary resistance strategies in non–civil war India, with logical remainders

India	c	f	EO1
Joda, post-2005 Sundargarh	0	1	0
Goa, Kudremukh, Bellary, Salem, Tiruvannamalai, Keonjhar (Banspal, etc.), Khandadhar (Sundargarh)	1	0	1

Outcome: 1

Number of implicants: 2

C   0   Goa, Kudremukh, Bellary, Salem, Tiruvannamalai, Keonjhar (Banspal, etc.), Khandadhar (Sundargarh)

F   0   Goa, Kudremukh, Bellary, Salem, Tiruvannamalai, Keonjhar (Banspal, etc.), Khandadhar (Sundargarh)

Number of solutions: 2

C
f

and not engaging in stakeholder dialogues were found to be necessary conditions for the Indian cases but not for all of the Brazilian cases. Brazil may have somewhat distinct dynamics, which could be assessed separately if one wants to find a minimal formula for what worked in that context. On the basis of the preceding comparisons, this is an important finding in and of itself.

Exclusion of the Brazilian cases did not result in the immediate finding of a meaningful minimal formula. Thereafter, by following the contextual logic, and on the basis of the prior identification of distinct contexts where strategies work differently, I next removed all of the Indian cases with a civil war context, as the use of arms radically influences how the other strategies might function. This resulted in a comparison across nine Indian cases. This iteration resulted in meaningful minimal formulas for explaining both when all mines are discontinued and when they are not.

Table 3.13 was produced using the Excel QCA tool developed by Cronqvist (2019). On the top it first sums up the cases that fall into the same category. Joda and post-2005 Sundargarh are cases without protests but with stakeholder dialogues directly with companies, which led to an agreement. In these cases, the mines were not shut down. In the other cases, a total of

84 How to apply QCA?

seven, the converse was true. When protests and abstention from private politics were used, mines were shut down or projects were discontinued. Table 3.13 has also calculated for the so-called "logical remainders," that is, cases that could logically be present in the database although they have not been observed. This is why the two solutions found imply that the outcome EO1 could be caused either by protesting or by avoiding private politics, as separate conditions. However, there is much controversy in QCA about whether logical remainders should be used because they introduce new epistemological problems, as they are based on a more statistical understanding in which all case variations would be possible in theory. In fact, the aforementioned search for parsimony has been criticized for producing false findings due to taking the Boolean logic beyond actually observed cases. Instead, an intermediate solution is suggested as the best way forward because, according to methodological comparisons, "A proper intermediate solution outperforms the parsimonious one in recovering a known causal structure and is positioned closest to the true, underlying causal model" (Duşa 2019, 21). On the bases of my own analysis and the technical analysis, I would avoid using the logical remainders tool, especially in ethnography-based analyses and especially if one has tried to collect a database with no nonobserved cases, as I did. I covered all of the major iron ore mining conflicts and projects in the two countries, and if a condition was not found, then I would not dare to take the step of assuming that it could be found as all meaningful cases were observed. In most studies, however, it is not possible to observe all meaningful cases or to compile a database without nonobserved cases. Thus, logical remainders could be used in other types of QCA applications (see Rihoux and De Meur 2009). They are also helpful in rethinking the database.

Table 3.14 was produced without the logical remainders.

Table 3.14 names the seven cases where, in order to reach EO1, both protesting and avoiding private politics had to be simultaneously present as causal conditions. The asterisk (*) between C and f in the solutions part of the table signifies the word "AND" in QCA. In formal QCA algorithms, a capital letter signifies that a causal condition has the value 1, and a lowercase letter signifies the value of 0. However, I have not followed this convention in this book but have instead expressed via writing if the causal condition (e.g., a strategy) was actively used. However, in the preceding truth tables that were produced by the Excel tool, the conventional signaling is used. I do recommend using it, especially if one is making more use of the QCA algorithms [which are not the focus here, partially because Collier (2014) and others have recommended avoiding the QCA algorithms in favor of simplicity].

A good QCA truth table exercise should test between four and seven conditions. In addition, to attain good results one should aim to include only

How to apply QCA? 85

Table 3.14 QCA truth table on necessary resistance strategies in non–civil war India

India	c	f EO1
Joda, post-2005 Sundargarh	0	1 0
Goa, Kudremukh, Bellary, Salem, Tiruvannamalai, Keonjhar (Banspal, etc.), Khandadhar (Sundargarh)	1	0 1

Outcome: 1NO

Number of implicants: 1

C*f   0   Goa, Kudremukh, Bellary, Salem, Tiruvannamalai, Keonjhar (Banspal, etc.), Khandadhar (Sundargarh)

Number of solutions: 1
C*f

conditions where at least one-third of the values given differ from the rest of the values (see Box 3.5. on "Good Practices" in Rihoux and De Meur 2009). For example, in my database of 22 cases, there should be at least seven cases that have the value of 0 or 1. The rest, in this case not more than 14, should have the other binary value. Next, I will do this exercise and remove all conditions from the list of 22 that do not fulfill this criterion. I ran this exercise for all 22 cases. This brought the number of strategy conditions down from ten to three (e2, e3, and g2). Of the seven outcomes observed, only one, EO1, fulfilled the variation requirement of at least eight cases differing from others in the set. Of the 12 contingency conditions, seven fulfilled the variation criteria (a1, a3, P2, P3, T2, CD1, and CD3). I then ran the QCA tool to see what a comparison of these ten conditions to EO1 yielded. This resulted in nine implicants, that is, configurations, that were related to mining discontinuation. These were individualized explanations, which is the reason the number of conditions had to be diminished. I started this process by considering which of the remaining ten factors could be thought to be important on the bases of theory and empirics. Thus, I removed condition a3 as it specified the context of resistance organization. T2 was also removed, because the factor of whether or not the ore was going to China did not surface as important for the resistance in these localities. I also removed P2, because during the global commodity supercycle, extractivism was expanding in many localities not just on the key national resource frontiers. Even with the removal of these factors, the result was still that the implicants were too individualized, although the number of conditions was down to seven. Thus, I also removed a1 and P3, leaving only the three resistance strategies and the two corporate strategies or actions for consideration. However, this comparison across five conditions did not lead to a single parsimonious explanation, as was expected. QCA has been criticized, for example, by Collier (2014) for the search for parsimony. Instead, he suggested a simpler usage of the method, and I concur with this critique. The truth tables I created fortified the findings of my prior analysis. This exercise suggests that in complex data sets based on ethnographic data across differing contexts, it is perhaps best to not even try to pursue a minimal formula. Instead, QCA-type analysis can be used in combination with probabilistic analysis, as demonstrated in the prior sections of this chapter. This can yield important insights into necessary and sufficient causalities across differing contexts, going far beyond what random comparisons across a multi-sited ethnography data set would allow.

The steps described herein are useful to identify factors that can be used in future QCA analysis and in other kinds of scoping and assessment of the identified factors. Ethnic relations and corporate agency emerged as important QCA causal conditions through the process described previously, and thus, the next chapter will explore these in more detail. The QCA truth table exercise was essential to highlight and identify that these factors are important and need to be studied further and to try to narrow down, rethink, or disaggregate the important factors to explain the outcomes of investment politics.

The exercise of identifying the five resistance strategies as sufficient was important for explaining discontinuation outcomes in India. I used this as a basis for the next step of my QCA. In this step, I first listed, in a new table, all the cases where all strategies a–e were active and f was inactive (A–F). I then merged these six strategies. If any of the three identified embedding tactics was used, it counted as use of the fifth strategy. If private politics were not used, this was counted as having a resistance movement that used the five key strategies while avoiding private politics. I use the shorthand of "peaceful radical contention" to denote this new causal condition, for which I created a new column in the overall Excel tool with all of my factors, labeled as A–F. I only performed this exercise for the 14 Indian cases. This resulted in five of the Indian cases having "peaceful radical contention." Next, I advanced step by step, adding other factors one at a time, to determine which results surged, starting from g1 and g2 and having EO1 as the outcome. This did not result in meaningful impacts as there were too many contradictory cases. I then assessed whether a1 and a3, together with A–F, could explain the outcomes. This produced Table 3.15.

How to apply QCA? 87

Table 3.15 illustrates that there were two solutions for explaining when all mining was discontinued in an area: Either all A–F were used as strategies or there was one unified movement that was backed by the local middle class resisting the expansion. This is marked by a plus sign (+) in the solutions section of the truth table. These were alternative paths, and the QCA exercise was useful in identifying that some of the contingency conditions could, on their own, offer an alternative and possibly more parsimonious explanation. Another key point illustrated by Table 3.15 is in the first line, which shows that there are four cases that are contradictory (marked with C). In all of these cases, a substantial part of the local population did not want mining to be stopped; rather, they wanted it to continue.

This made me rethink of the importance of identifying the goals of the locals in the given investment area. Did most of them want the mines to close or not? This type of questioning goes back to one of the original questions that every researcher should consider. What are you trying to say and about what? In other words, what is this case about? There are several subsets of answers that come to mind. Next, it is worth separating the cases in a new way by including only those cases in the studied set where there was a clear resistance actor that wanted mining to be discontinued in the region

Table 3.15 Exploring for alternative explanations of investment outcomes through QCA

India	A–F	a1	a3	EO1
Bellary, Joda, post-2005 Sundargarh, Manpur	0	0	0	C
West Singhbhum, Dantewada	0	0	1	0
Salem, Keonjhar (Banspal, etc.)	0	1	0	1
Dalli Rajhara	0	1	1	0
Khandadhar (Sundargarh), Rowghat	1	0	1	1
Goa, Kudremukh, Tiruvannamalai	1	1	1	1

Outcome: 1

Number of implicants: 2

A–F	0	Khandadhar (Sundargarh), Rowghat, Goa, Kudremukh, Tiruvannamalai
A1*a3	0	Salem, Keonjhar (Banspal, etc.)

Number of solutions: 1

A–F + A1*a3

and no other, clearly competing, civil society groups advocating for another type of solution to mining (e.g., continuation, slowing down, compensation). This resulted in a table with eight to nine cases: Goa, Kudremukh, Tiruvannamalai, Keonjhar (Banspal, etc.), Khandadhar (Sundargarh), Rowghat, Apolo, and possibly also Minas-Rio. Several insights could be drawn by comparing the causal conditions to the outcomes across this set of cases where the locals resisted mining and wanted to discontinue both its existing and planned operations. First, in all but one case (Minas-Rio), the outcome was discontinuation (EO1). This is a remarkable outcome and indicates the importance of resistance adequately framing what it wants and having a unified local reaction in response to a policy. Second, the outlier case of Minas-Rio is interesting, and I will discuss that case more in detail. I did not do field research in this locality myself, yet this comparison suggests that there is a need to go to that area and perform a more detailed analysis, as it seems to be a highly interesting outlier case that can reveal something important about overall dynamics. I share more about this later.

I explored the necessary and sufficient conditions to explain the eight cases where mines were discontinued. I did this through a QCA comparison of all of the strategy and contingency conditions. The results showed that protesting and avoiding private politics were the necessary and sufficient conditions to explain when mining was discontinued in these cases, as they all shared these two conditions. No other condition was shared across all the cases, which suggests that the contingencies are not as important as the two strategies of protesting and making private deals with corporations, which had already been identified as necessary conditions earlier in the analysis. The more precise comparison across cases where resistance actually desired closures showed how crucial these two strategies were. They provide a sufficiently parsimonious explanation. Thereafter, this path of QCA calibration led to an important outcome: A minimal formula to explain how, when, and what kind of resistance succeeded in investment politics.

The Minas-Rio discrepancy I mentioned previously led me to ask a Brazilian research assistant who is highly knowledgeable about the area to express her opinions and viewpoints on my classifications of the case. This is a form of researcher triangulation. This researcher triangulation was the best path to take, as the global pandemic made it impossible for me to travel to the locality. I had long telephone conversations with my research assistant, who spent several months in the area gaining insider knowledge on the dynamics of the Minas-Rio project, including opening up all the causal conditions and outcomes. She supported the inclusion of all of them for analysis and offered extremely valuable insights on how to sharpen some of them to assist in pinpointing the particularities of this case. When I asked if the tables illuminate the most important dynamics, she agreed and also suggested a couple of new factors to be considered in future research. At

How to apply QCA? 89

my request, the assistant sent the QCA tables for the Minas-Rio case to be filled in by several key activists and community members, as well as people linked to the company. In this exercise, these key players filled in the QCA tables with their judgments on what should be given a 0 and what should be given a 1. I compared their responses to my original QCA tables. This co-creation of knowledge generated a better understanding and assessment of what the situation was like in 2005–2015 because these reflections were from people who knew the situation well and because by 2020 new evidence had emerged since I did my initial research in 2010–2016. As a result of these efforts, a new row was created for Minas-Rio, where some of the values changed. These reflections help to showcase how a researcher using QCA should be transparent in the choices they have made, especially in opening up the research process and the steps taken to sharpen the analysis, instead of just presenting the final results. This kind of analysis should be provided in a methodological appendix to provide transparency and opportunity for deeper reflection on how the choice between a causal condition or outcome was deemed to be 1 or 0 in a specific case. This is also important in other types of QCA, where it would be something between in the case of fuzzy-logic analysis (from 0 to 1) or values over 1 in the case of multi-value analysis, based on the researcher's methodological choices.

Transparent recalibration of QCA results from a distance

Two key findings were uncovered in 2020 when I asked others for comments on the Minas-Rio valuations that I had created in 2015–2016. These tables were based on the information available from a distance (as I could not travel due to the pandemic) and my discussions and interviews between 2011 and 2015 with scholars and others knowledgeable about the case. The first finding was that after some years passed and more information came out, the values in the QCA tables should be revisited, as they might change as a result of the new data.

Table 3.16 presents the recalibrated csQCA values for the Minas-Rio case, based on new information obtained in 2020. As a reminder, I have added the old values to the table, which were set in 2015–2016 based on the information available at that time.

Interestingly, 8 of the 29 values observed changed in the reevaluation. This begs for at least a quick reassessment of the key truth table findings and minimal formulas. Thus, I reassessed the data based on this new information concerning the Minas-Rio case, which was a discrepant case before, to see whether better general patterns emerge. It is important to note that even one case where the values were not estimated as well as possible might result in problems for the whole QCA research and its findings. Even though the reality of complex, multi-sited research is that one cannot observe all

Table 3.16 Recalibrated values for the Minas-Rio case (2005–2015) based on new information obtained in 2020

Strategies	Outcomes	Contingencies

a	b	c	d	e1	e2	e3	f	g1	g2	EO1	EO2	EO3	PO1	PO2	PO3	PO4	a1	a2	a3	P1	P2	P3	T1	T2	GE1	CD1	CD2	CD3

Minas-Rio 2005–2015 (new values, based on information available in 2020)

| 0 | 0 | 1 | 0 | 0 | 0 | 0 | 1 | 0 | 0 | 0 | 0 | 1 | 0 | 0 | 0 | 0 | 0 | 0 | 0 | 1 | 1 | 1 | 0 | 0 | 0 | 0 | 1 | 1 |

Minas-Rio 2005–2015 (old values, based on information available in 2016)

| 1 | 1 | 1 | 0 | 1 | 0 | 0 | 0 | 0 | 0 | 0 | 1 | 0 | 1 | 1 | 0 | 0 | 0 | 0 | 0 | 1 | 0 | 1 | 1 | 0 | 1 | 0 | 1 | 0 |

the cases as well or in as much detail, the goal should still be to provide analysis without nonobserved cases. The probabilistic approach suggested earlier seems to be a promising pathway because it can diminish the impact of cases that have not been observed well enough so that they do not make an inaccurate contribution to the whole.

The most important table that I needed to update to reflect the new information on Minas-Rio was Table 3.5, which presented the impact of peaceful resistance by the simultaneous use of all the strategies a–e. This table helped to explain when the resistance was successful in attaining its goals, assuming that this occurred when a–e were all used. Before, the cases of Minas-Rio, Carajás (old), and Corumbá were the only ones where all of the strategies a–e were used but mining was not discontinued. The latter two cases can now be explained by the fact that the goal of the resistance in these areas was not even the discontinuation of all mining, all projects, or both in the area. I identified this in the minimal formula exercise earlier. Minas-Rio can now be explained without the use of all strategies a–e as resistance strategies, as the prior notions on resistance styles and strengths were overestimations. Minas-Rio can thus be dropped from Table 3.5. This makes the support for the key hypothesis much more robust. This example demonstrates how one can and should use the primary logic of elimination though QCA to find out what causal condition configurations best explain the outcomes that are of the most interest. In all cases where the resistance used the five key strategies (a–e) and aimed to discontinue mining, the goal was attained when comparing all iron ore mining cases in Brazil and India. However, it should be noted explicitly that Brazil did not have any such cases where all of a–e were used and resistance aimed for and managed to stop mining. So, one cannot definitively say whether the use of a–e would result in outcomes similar to those in India. Nevertheless, the recalibration of results proved to be an important test and is highly recommended. This can be done when the causal conditions and outcomes are clearly laid out and explained, as in the preceding tables, so the people who receive them can understand them without the need for further explanations.

The other finding was that one needs to create distinct tables for distinct time periods or use a temporal QCA to perform a temporal analysis [see Ragin and Strand (2008) for this as I will not go into detail about this method]. Besides asking people to evaluate what the 2005–2015 period looked like for Minas-Rio in 2020 and recalibrating the table based on that new information, I also asked these people to fill in another row for the situation at Minas-Rio as they assessed it to be in 2019–2020. The situation described in 2019–2020 was quite different from that in 2005–2015, which showed that the dynamics of Minas-Rio had changed considerably. I will not go into detail here, but this short example shows how one could also make use of QCA to perform a longitudinal analysis by breaking the period studied into different, shorter periods. These subdivided periods could then be used for investigating and explaining how things had changed and why, on the basis of the QCA tables produced. This could be done for a number of cases, but in that research design, I would keep the number of field sites much more limited than in this research. This type of longitudinal analysis could yield very interesting comparisons, for example, about the role of polity transformation, because since 2005–2015 both India and Brazil have transitioned from consolidating democracy (see Kröger 2020) to a markedly more authoritarian populism. Thus, one could use a comparison of the post-2015 period across these cases to determine how the place-based, micropolitics of resistance had transformed since that polity shift.

Summary

A QCA-oriented approach is helpful to identify cases that need to be explored further and to ensure that all cases receive the attention they deserve. The best approach would be to carry out all field research oneself. Yet, in a very large, multi-sited ethnographic research project like this one, it can become crucial to also rely on other information and a team of researchers. In the next chapter, I will further discuss the results obtained through my more detailed ethnographic research and many other forms of triangulation to explore the particularities of key causalities.

The technical analysis in this chapter explored different aspects of the csQCA methodology. The chapter showcased how consolidated, more focused tables are easier to follow than bigger ones and how they offer detailed information about specific factors and their relations to outcomes. As we have seen, the QCA tables allow us to view with some precision the linkages between resistance strategies and economic and political outcomes, along with the significance of various contingencies. Next, I will expand on some of the contingencies described earlier in more detail, as the dynamics can be quite abstract if they remain only on the level of QCA descriptions. The following discussion section will be helpful to better understand the role of factors other than resistance strategies in investment politics, that is, how complex causalities need to be opened up in good research by means other than just QCA truth tables and their analysis.

Notes

1 http://ejatlas.org/conflict/corumba-indigenous-communities-and-mining-brazil (accessed August 13, 2015).
2 Many Corumbá projects and mines—all of which are small—have been closed or suspended by market forces since 2013 (http://af.reuters.com/article/energy OilNews/idAFE5N0P705920141205).

3 The Justice MB Shah Commission was appointed in November 2010 to probe the illegal mining of iron and manganese ores in contravention of provisions of the Mines and Minerals (Development and Regulation) Act (1957), the Forest (Conservation) Act (1980), and the Environment (Protection) Act (1986). By the time the government ended the Commission's tenure in October 2013, its investigations had "led to the closure of hundreds of illegal mines" (www.tehelka.com/who-is-the-mines-ministry-trying-to-save/, accessed June 30, 2015). These outcomes were not a result of the Commission per se, as civil society activism was crucial in forging the Commission.
4 In mining industry terminology, greenfield refers to new mining areas that are opened; whereas, brownfield refers to the expansion of already-existing mining sites or reopening of an old mining area.
5 The Maoists typically deny claims that they have received money from companies not to close mines, for example, in the case of Dantewada (see http://Naxalrevolution.blogspot.fi/2012/06/oppose-army-deployment-in-bastar.html accessed August 7, 2015).
6 Corumbá can be said to have failed because, in this case, strategy f was used. All movements in the overall database that used strategy f failed to obtain EO1—due to a different assortment of causal conditions, of course—but in the case of Corumbá, the crucial role of strategy f as "a kiss of death" to resistance ambitions was the clearest.

4 Complementing QCA by a detailed opening of explanatory factors

Chapter Abstract: *This chapter shows how the most important factors studied can and should be explored, not just through a condensed analysis in QCA tables (as in Chapter 3) but also in a more extended form. The chapter will lead the reader through the process of revealing the role of the factors that do not fit neatly into QCA tables via process tracing and ethnographically based analysis. This kind of analysis should complement a good comparative analysis, even though they are not always done in conjunction. By focusing theoretically on social movement studies and political ecology, this chapter provides examples of the empirical analyses that complement QCA and what are behind them. This chapter also explains how all of the aforementioned five key strategies are not always available for would-be resistances to use, for example, if they are in an ethnically marginalized position or are without other backing like the support of the urban middle classes or critical mining professionals. Both these broader contextual factors and dynamics are such that they require exploration of how they affect the QCA conditions.*

Focused on contingency factors, this chapter will be especially helpful for determining to what extent the lessons concerning iron ore investment politics in Brazil and India can be generalized. The prior chapter showed how the impact of resistance strategies must be studied in the political dynamics and context in which they are used. This chapter probes the impact of other factors on investment outcomes, including ethnic relations (e.g., the displacement of forest-based minorities by social elites), third parties (e.g., foreign governments, competing capitalists), and the style of corporate agency (e.g., public versus private, large versus small capital, corporate outreach). There are many other important factors that could be considered, but I selected the role of ethnic relations and corporate or third-party actors as worthy of detailed examination, as these discussions demonstrate how QCA truth table analysis, which can be quite complex, should be expanded through a more detailed analysis. A focus on ethnicity and what could be characterized as the pushing side of extractivism also helps to expose the wider context in which iron ore extraction takes place, that is, the role of investment politics overall. It is not sufficient to only study resistance strategies because these are not crafted in a void and because even having the ability to build effective resistance strategies is more of a possibility for some social groups than others, as different groups are pressured either less or more by those wanting to extract resources. This chapter exemplifies how QCA should be followed by broader theoretical discussions and analyses that situate the findings. I will first study the role of ethnic relations, after which I will focus on the role of corporate agency and third parties.

Describing ethnographies of complex interactions and outcomes

The case of Minas-Rio showcases the many factors that should be considered when reporting on and analyzing complex cases and their outcomes. I also include a temporal analysis, as the dynamics have changed since the early 2010s when I originally observed the case. Since then, there have been two major tailings dam ruptures that caused massive catastrophes in the state of Minas Gerais and elsewhere in Brazil. New research has also been published on the ethnography of the region, which was not available in 2010. For example, Santos, Ferreira, and Penna (2017) provide an ethnography of how the Anglo American mining company used questionable methods to force the project's environmental licensing through, although the affected communities heavily resisted this operation for years. The project has led to violence and many different types of violations of rights, which are assessed by Prates (2017). Prates details how at the same time, however, a resistance movement was consolidated that led roadblock protests in 2016 (after the period I studied) under the banner of a movement called REAJA (Rede de Articulacao e Justica dos Atingidos do Projeto Minas-Rio, the Network of Articulation and Justice of People Affected by the Minas Rio Project). This resistance has mainly taken actions such as documenting violations by photographing and sharing the photos, not signing documents of the company or participating in its meetings, planting and collecting wood on company lands, and other daily tactics that Prates (2017, 107) characterizes as "weapons of the weak," following the conceptualization by Scott (2008). The accounts by Santos and Prates provide further information to use for evaluating the context and trajectory to explain the relatively weak resistance and the sophisticated corporate countertactics. In addition to this new research, the information here is based on my old data and on new telephone interviews conducted in May 2020 with people knowledgeable about the region.

According to the informants, the ways of life are set by the Anglo American company in the Conceição de Mato Dentro city, which is the headquarters of the Minas-Rio project. They have 3,000–4,000 workers living in the small town. The colonial city dates back to the 18th century and has generally had conservative values. The past of the city is still present with the characteristics of a slave-ownership mentality. My informants alleged that there is racism present in the white middle classes and very conservative elites. Life in the city seems to be affected on many levels by the company. All of the workers have to observe the rule of not making noise in the historic city, and if they do, people can denounce them. The setting is quite specific, and it is difficult and probably not useful to place all of these particular factors as causal conditions for QCA because the other cases would not show these specific values.

However, it is possible to place these specifics under more generic explanatory and outcome factors, and this is what I did in the previous demonstrations. However, it is essential to explain these key particularities further so as to not lose them in the course of running the QCA. For example, the corporate countertactics have become ever more sophisticated through time. The company has created a specific committee for community relations, and it has hired many important former activists and experts as employees. These committee members negotiate the removal of affected people from the zones of operation, for example, under the dams. This committee is also where people can leave their complaints about the mining company. According to an insider informant, Anglo enforces very strong rules for its workers and the professionals offering services.

My informants, who are familiar with contexts throughout Brazil, emphasized their experience with what they described as the peculiarity of the context in Minas-Rio. The quotes in the forthcoming section come from the telephone interviews I conducted and reflect the impressions that my informants have about their lived experiences with Minas-Rio. What follows is a description of the context, based on their impressions. This type of description could be utilized in the presentation of QCA research to help highlight the nuances collected via ethnographic techniques.

The informants describe the area as isolated, without resources, and as a very "backward society" of old elites. It is a rural community without proper access to schools. Locals give examples of children that need to walk 5 km to reach the road where the school bus passes. I was told how the countryside consists of very poor people who live by selling their labor on a day-to-day basis to the region's small farms, which are described as "very oppressive." The informants told me the area is marked by "very strong racial oppression," as the region has several Afro-descended Quilombo communities, whose ancestors escaped slavery and established their own rural communities, yet are still downtrodden today. In this setting, my informants characterized land conflicts as "serious," and they told me that members of the Quilombo community had been killed in land conflicts even before the mining project.

It was said that the environmental problems in the area increased as the mining project advanced. There were claims of dust entering the houses and people unable to garden due to the pollution. Meanwhile, there was talk that the people in the town who owned land are now millionaires because they sold their land to the company. The Secretary of the Environment for the municipality was said to be one of these people, as they had sold their family farm during this time period.

When speaking to my informants on the telephone, I asked them to specifically reflect on the factors in the QCA table, which I had sent to them beforehand. They were instructed to place their own valuations into the tables, and then we discussed their conceptualization of the tables. This was an extremely fruitful exercise, and I recommend adopting this method in all QCA-based research, especially in studies based on ethnographic material. This process allows the researcher to go back and forth between analysis and concept creation and the empirical realities. I will next discuss the factors where the prior values differed from the informants' values and explain how these discussions helped to crystalize what was important in these factors.

(a) The prior table showed that the Minas-Rio case had a mass social movement organizing and politicizing in the region. This was challenged. The two key, national, mining-critical networks, the Movement of People Affected by Dams (MAB) and the Movement for Popular Sovereignty over Mining (MAM), "never had people in the region," while the community "kind of tried to resist a little bit," but eventually the community was "co-opted by money." The resistance to Minas-Rio that started in 2010 was based principally on the activism by public prosecutors and NGOs, not by local people. The leadership was made up not of the local people but of progressive state and NGO actors. Key local leaders were assassinated, and thus the mobilization waned.

(b) The region has a notable presence of Quilombo communities based on Afro-spiritual religious practices and ontologies of nature, which are drastically different in comparison to the elite's religious beliefs and ways of relating to nature. However, due to strong, prevailing ethnic discrimination, these communities do not openly express that they are worried about the saint or spirit in a river being destroyed by mining, but rather that they are worried about losing their land. This translates their nonmodernist framing to a modern framing. Quilombos have a distinct understanding of nature in comparison to other environmentalists. Oxum lives in the waterfalls, which are sacred areas, and therefore there cannot be mining in these regions.[1] When Quilombos resist mining, they defend their whole way of life, wherein this cosmology is part of the particular relation to work, a place to live, life itself, and the particular religiosity of Umbanda. These are all spaces outside of a physical church, but within the Quilombo territory spirituality is also present in the waterfalls and tree trunks. They defend these against mining, as well as their gardens and houses, all of their territory with its existing relations. However, what appears to many outsiders is that their resistance is the same as elsewhere around rural Brazilian land conflicts. The ontological specificities are translated in a transmodern translation process into the general category of local defense of their existing territory. However, this defense of territory as an overall category hides important distinctions on which the struggle is actually based. In the Brazilian context, traditional populations refers to the rural populations that have lived for long periods in particular places and have developed identities based on particular livelihoods rooted in those places (such as rubber tapper, riverside dweller, artisanal fisher, nut collector, and so on) They have at least somewhat similar, nonmodernist understandings of their territories as indigenous groups and the Afro-Brazilian communities described previously (see Kröger and Lalander 2016). However, as this would cause discrimination in "Brazil's atmosphere of dire religious prejudice"—as Brazil's current state of affairs was characterized by one informant—this is hidden and not shown openly in their resistance campaigns.

There is a different way of understanding the world that is shared among the majority of the affected people and also among the non-Quilombo peasants. For these long-term rural dwellers, the value of life is measured differently, more through their own work and sweat on their particular piece of land. It is difficult to measure these values in monetary terms, and as a result, the older people have a very strong relation and attachment to these spaces. Often, younger people find that the loss of land can be compensated by a certain amount of money. They see that the land is like some other land elsewhere and can accept a certain amount of compensation for selling it. In 2020, the debate in Minas-Rio revolved "around financial value," and the politics focused on financial compensation. Others want Anglo to resolve the problems, such as water accessibility, and if this was done they would not want to leave. Currently, most inhabitants do want to leave because of the pollution and conflicts. Yet, an NGO called Nucleus of Assistance to Communities Affected by Dams (NACAB) is currently campaigning to mobilize the people to resist. In support of resistance, they are building on the understanding of the right to use land, which permeates throughout Brazil. This has been the most important basis for campaigning in mining and other rural conflicts.

These discussions were extremely helpful to help clarify what is meant by modernist and nonmodernist campaigning in the context of Brazil and how this should be measured across cases. In practice, the same rule for assessing whether protesting was present in a case can be adopted for observing campaigning that challenges the logic of financial compensation. If a protest is not noted by the main media and powerholders, it does not count as a protest. Likewise, if a campaigning frame does not explicitly argue, for example, that there are spirits living in a certain waterfall, then this is not nonmodernist campaigning. Thereafter, I estimated that b was not used as a strategy in Minas-Rio. However, I would add another specificity to strategy b in future studies. I would articulate a new specificity: Values that go beyond the monetary compensation of an area, that is, the kind of peasant understanding of their territory that the older generation had, and campaigning based on this noncompensatory, nonmonetary approach to land.

(c, d and e) The reobservation of these factors through researcher triangulation (key informant discussions) and letting time pass so that the case could be reobserved after five years led to a sharpened understanding of agentive dynamics and their importance. One should also make sure to note the scale of action and the origin of the key actors and agents in a complex situation (e.g., locality), as this is important information for making sense of the outcomes. Protests were organized by the locals, and these were noted in the Minas-Rio case until 2015. However, networking wherein the locals created networks and reached out to other places did not occur according to the reevaluation. State embedding also was not used by the local resistance. This area continues to be a typical Brazilian region where vote-buying occurs; thus, the electoral politics were not transformed. The autonomy of the resistance was not maintained through a self-agentive process. This resistance was a top-down rather than a grassroots mobilization based on the creation of new institutional arrangements. The outsider NGOs and state actors tried to boost the local identities and resistance in a setting where the resistance "dies without the presence of the state and others." However, things started to change in this regard after the NACAB NGO entered the area in 2019. For example, important legal victories were won for the locals in 2020.[2]

The other key differences that were found in the distance recalibration could also have been found by a field research trip to the locality if the global situation allowed for safe travel. The community had already compromised and enmeshed with the private politics of the company through direct monetary compensation without state presence. Both poor and middle-class residents were selling their land and making deals with the mining company. The town was also an important ecotourism hub, and this sector resisted mining in its own way. This resistance was based in the local middle class, the same people who had sold their land to the mining company. They wanted to put a limit on further expansion, but they did not oppose the mining itself. This opposition was and still is not expressed openly, as there are no open actions or visible support for the local rural communities that are losing water and land access. This is rather a "resistance of the rich," which obtained money from the company for a park and which helps the municipality behind the scenes in negotiations with the company for other public works.

(GE1) Another interesting factor was that in 2020, it was possible to see that the prior estimation of the excellent iron ore grade had to be downgraded because it became clear that the iron content was about 40%, not over 60% as had been marketed to Anglo American. This shows the political character and uncertainty of the numeric factors of the geographical data and highlights the need for detailed scrutiny of the quality of statistical or numerical data obtained from other sources. This type of data also needs to be rigorously examined through triangulation.

(CD3) The corporate countertactics against potential resistance have developed through the years, becoming "supersophisticated." Specific sectors have been established, and professionals are hired for community relations. According to an internal informant, there are now three professionals for each affected community. Regular meetings are held with communities each month, and the company has taken a leading role in the formation of careers for locals. The company has even established a technical school in the municipality, and now "all the children of the community want to work for Anglo."

I also asked my informants if anything should be added to the long list of over 20 causal factors. They first said no, that the list was good, covered the key issues well, and should be used for future studies on similar topics. However, after I pressed for more additions, three factors were mentioned. First, the number of jobs created by the investment in relation to the community size should be compared across the cases, as this could have a potential impact on the overall dynamics and outcomes. This led me to think that if one included this measure, mvQCA or fsQCA might be a good option instead of csQCA. Second, one should observe whether there are other options for work in the locality where there is investment (this can be a yes or no option). The Minas-Rio locality does not have other options for many work categories in comparison to the state capital and, thus, "Anglo is almost a hero." Ecotourism provides very few jobs, mostly in small hotels. Thus, it does make a difference if the targeted town is small or large, as the middle classes seem to play a key role. Third, one should note whether there is basic infrastructure in the locality. For example, if roads and schools are missing and the investing company promises to build these, this "breaks the resistance." If the company starts to perform the role of the public power, "then it manages to do whatever it wants." These three factors should be taken into consideration in future studies on investment politics.

This section has illustrated how one can produce a more detailed description of a complex setting where the dynamics change and where the valuation of key factors is also prone to change as time passes and as more detailed information becomes available. I have demonstrated how one should detail the QCA factors and revisit and reconsider them, which adds to one's understanding of and ability to engage with theory making. Next, I will continue to expand upon the role of contextual factors revealed by ethnographic research, but which may seem difficult to render in their totality in QCA logic. This showcases how particularly interesting and important dynamics should be given more attention in writing based on field research findings and how they should be observed via QCA, including how one should explain the reasons for setting the factors.

Opening up complex social relations: ethnic relations and resource politics

Next, I will illustrate a type of analysis that further expands the QCA-based evaluations of situations by providing textual descriptions and analysis of contextual and contingency matters. The contingencies of ethnicity and ethnic relations need to be assessed to understand complex interactions studied via ethnography, such as extractivism. This is because there is a strong ethnic component in many mining conflicts, as industrial-scale mining has been principally an initiative led by Western colonialism over the course of world history.[3] There is often a complex mix of different types of politics in violent resource extraction areas, including the politics of indigeneity and nationalism, as well as rifts and power relations within the local groups [see, e.g., Watts (2004) on the Niger Delta]. These dynamics were also prominent in my database. An ethnicized, unequal control over underground resources is inherent in many countries' extractivism [e.g., in Colombia, see Vélez-Torres (2014)]. It should be noted that the role of interethnic relations in explaining political opportunities, mobilization, dynamics of contention, and outcomes is not straightforward. However, there are some general tendencies, which I will discuss in this section.

Ethnic injustices were a marked feature in many of the cases I studied. I identified 14 cases out of the 23 with "a deep ethnic injustice" (contingency factor P3 in the QCA analysis). P3 refers to mining that represents profound ethnic injustice by benefiting mostly elite ethnic groups and perpetrating forestland loss that affects mostly vulnerable communities (e.g., indigenous groups). The conflict cases that had the most severe forms of violence, such as armed conflicts, were included in the P3 category. Thus, there seemed to be a caveat for resistance by ethnic minorities, which may drive them toward a more limited set of strategies. At my request, the leader of a Bhubaneshwar-based human rights NGO reflected on the difference of Goa and Odisha (also called Orissa) from the socioethnic perspective (interview, March 8, 2013):

> In Orissa there are more movements and more violence than in Goa. Goa is a smaller place and there are more literate, more educated people. Goa is a more cosmopolitan place. There are people from different countries. In Orissa mostly people are tribals, less literate people. But movements are empowered.

In Brazil and India, ethnic background and class are closely correlated (Guzmán 2013; Omvedt 2011). In Brazil, the urban middle classes are typically from the majority ethnic background and have better connections to the state than ethnic minority communities, such as the Afro-Brazilian Quilombolas, traditional populations, indigenous people, or other rural poor (Kröger 2013).[4] Indigenous peoples have had to render up their lands for extraction, typically after violence, to feed white settler populations, as mining itself was historically the task of slaves of African origin or indigenous people.

In my database, different types of alliances and rifts between local resistance groups also surfaced, and they manifested as cross-class, interethnic, and intersector. I compared how these specificities in local resistance group formation related to outcomes. In several places, many resistance groups work independently for the same goal. However, these groups come from different constituencies, that is, they are from different classes, castes, or ethnic groups. To conduct a QCA that relates resistance formation to outcomes in such a setting, I identified the specificity in the context of resistance organization as contingency factor a3. An interesting and important finding from my QCA analysis is that a topography of several cross-class and cross-caste movements may work more effectively than a single large movement in uniting all the different strands of activism. The economic outcomes were generally more impressive in the 11 cases with a3 than in the other cases, although there were a few anomalies where a3 clearly did not support the resistance to extractivism, perhaps because of the quality of a3 in these cases, a point I will return to later. The conventional logic would be that the bigger and more united the movement, the better. However, analysis of these cases in comparative terms suggests that the more numerous the concordant movements, the greater the impact—the proviso being that each movement should also be heterogeneous in order to avoid caste- or class-based violence and racism. This is a novel claim. Such a topography was present in Goa, where the movement was split into two major resistance movements. One movement had more upper-caste activists (alongside Adivasis and others) from poor and wealthy backgrounds and urban and rural areas, while the other was led more strongly by Adivasis and Dalits, but still included other castes and classes (interviews, 2010–2014). Likewise, in Kudremukh, hostile movements came together in their resistance to the mine, but after the mine was closed by their efforts, they resumed their hostilities (that is, between the Adivasis, environmentalists, and peasants). A separation of these actors was beneficial in order to gather their particular constituencies for the united struggle. There were also other cases in India that followed these dynamics of contention but only one case in Brazil, suggesting that interculturalism allows movements to network more comprehensively in Brazil and that communalist multiculturalism makes such attempts difficult in India.[5]

Several of my Indian informants argued that there are potential pitfalls of having an intercaste resistance group. It may be difficult and counterproductive to bring together different castes into one united movement. The QCA analysis revealed that in those areas where movements were led not by Adivasis but by outsiders, there was a far greater possibility of resistance failure. In this analysis, I studied the period between 2005 and 2015 and used different materials from that period to explain the dynamics. The following analysis draws from publications and information during that period. In the most heavily mined area of Odisha, Keonjhar's Joda block, the local Adivasis had been "protesting" for decades peacefully and nonviolently against mining expansion, according to HNF (HOTnHIT Newsfeatures), an Odisha-based "media action centre." However, these acts were not noted by the authorities, the media, or the public at large. In old mining settings, where the non-mining-based lived environments have already been ravaged and Adivasis displaced, there is typically less resistance. According to an activist from Joda, "there is no resistance."[6] The movement that did exist was taken over by non-Adivasis, who urged the Adivasis to take poorly remunerated mining jobs instead of resisting. Ethnic relations are central to explaining why the resistance in Joda was meager and led to disappointment for the locals, whose only wish was to retain their land (Baverstock n.d., 69).[7] Many Adivasis have no other option than to turn to Maoist armed resistance if they wish to retain their land at any price.

In Joda, the local leaders have opted to avoid violence and urge using private politics (strategy f), instead of either forging peaceful resistance using the concatenated strategies a–e (which worked in the neighboring Keonjhar blocks in stalling mine expansions) or joining in the Maoist insurgency (which would have been easy for them, given the proximity of the West

Singhbhum Maoist stronghold). These Adivasis, with a markedly nondevelopmentalist, nonmodernist, and noncapitalist culture and livelihood, are not accepted as members of the Indian democracy, which is an industrial complex of steel and hydrocarbons like other modern democracies (see Mitchell 2011; Livingston 2019). This is the first, major ethnic dimension that puts them at odds with mining. Additionally, nontribal, prodevelopment people have occupied leadership positions and, via these second-level ethnic relations, have had the power to convince people not to mount a resistance strong enough to have any effect.

Otherness can be used to legitimize violence, particularly against those who are framed as profane and/or ethnically inferior.[8] As an illustration, Baviskar (2001, 375) notes that in India elements of tribal culture, including the freedom women have to select a husband and to divorce, have become "a convenient device to fix and explain violence, to routinize it." In Brazil, the intercultural cleavage between the indigenous peoples and the majority has severe, built-in barriers that do not allow tribal culture to become a political device for routinizing violence (into a two-sided armed conflict with quite crisp ethnic cleavage lines) as easily or as widely as in India. Initially, this is because ethnic-cultural lines are much more blurred (than in the Indian caste system), and indigeneity has been a legitimate part of the multicultural self-image of Brazilian nationhood. Current politicization by Brazilian indigenous movements considers them to be simultaneously native and national (Guzmán 2013), a position that does not differ from the self-perceptions of the majority of Indian Adivasis. Most importantly, indigenous mobilization in Brazil has a different quality than that in India. In Brazil, unlike in India, indigenous groups have networked better with other constituents, like the landless workers of La Via Campesina. Brazilian activists have the advantage of not having mobilized on isolated ethnic lines but have already relied for decades on a Latin American tradition of *mestizajem*, or ethnic mixing, which results in more equal interethnic relations in Brazil than in India. Such intercultural mixing, creating a new national identity where hybrid cultures are considered a positive, is a boost for creating interethnic alliances and avoiding ethnically based violence. There are also no religious schisms in Brazil as in India. Brazilians often have no problem visiting or being part of several different congregations at the same time.[9] Such underlying metacultural differences and how they shape the organization of cultural differences within a given context seem to be an important factor, which could be examined in more detail in future studies.

This section has discussed how particularities in the politics of ethnicity and nationalism show variations based on the underlying metacultures of Brazil and India, which shape the quality of ethnic relations. Several particular causal conditions were identified for systematic QCA analysis through my focus on the role of ethnic relations. I provided a wider account of these factors, not all of which could be converted to a QCA study. An underlying tendency that requires more in-depth scrutiny is the role of metapolitics, including imbuing nature with greater agency.

Now, I will turn the discussion to study of the role of corporate agency and third parties, which also emerged as key contingencies on the basis of the literature review and field research, in addition the other factors of ethnicity, geography, the regional ecology and sector of extractivism, and temporality. The relations between corporate agency, third parties, and resistance are interactive, and it is essential to provide an analysis of these dynamics.

Analyzing international relations and a multitude of actors through QCA: corporate agency and third parties' roles as examples

A coordinator of an NGO in Keonjhar, Odisha, explained to me how the local Adivasis see the corporate agency of mining:

> Adivasis say companies are like monkeys. You will take them out, they will come again. Again, take them out, again they will come. Again, leave them out, again they will come. So, Adivasi people say they are monkeys. They come again and again and again like monkeys. So, we cannot assume that they are gone because their interest is that they need property. They will come again and again and again. They will cast people anywhere. Other times they will come with police or they will come with military or they will come with government to take our land.

Mining investment outcomes are typically seen as depending much more on corporate decisions, state actions, and the role of third parties (customers and markets) than on resistance efforts. In this section, I observe how the actions and compositions of these three factors have influenced the causal impact of resistance on outcomes. In many mining settings, the roles of states are so merged with mining industry expansion that this thrust can be studied under the single title of "corporate agency," which covers both.

According to a former Minister of Finance of the Madhya Pradesh state whom I interviewed (Chhattisgarh was part of this state before 2000), in India illegal and legal mining is perpetrated by both politicians and the business elite, which are "all mixed up." Sometimes corporations have either captured or strongly embedded the state and state actors are the key corporations, creating a corporate nexus or an exclusive corporate-state form of "encompassing embeddedness" (see Evans 1995, 2010). Besides corporate agency, which is most visible in the investments by large corporations such as Vale, POSCO, Vedanta, SAIL, BHP Billiton, Tata, and Jindal—their projects form the bulk of cases in Indian and Brazilian iron ore politics—there is also an extractivist agency that operates, at least on the ground, primarily via the logic of "artisanal" or small-scale mining, such as placer mining. This small-scale mining is far more common for gold and other precious metals than for iron ore, although there was also significant extractivism based on small-scale, nonestablished looting taking place during the iron ore scam in areas such as a Goa, Bellary, and Odisha. I heard stories of wanton groups of men coming overnight with a truck and an excavator to grab iron ore from rich deposit areas and to then sell it to the corporations exporting the ore or to steel plants. Even though such operations might not be directly referred to as corporate agency (rather, they are some other type of extractivist agency), their operations are still subsumed under the larger capitalist logic, which is dominated by corporate agency, and under that agency's profit-making logic and logistical chains. For this reason, the concept of corporate agency can capture most of the extractivist pushes at least in the cases studied in this book.

There is case-specific variation in this corporate agency, which depends, for example, on the following contingencies I studied via QCA: Company size (analyzed as corporate agency difference CD2 in the QCA, identifying large and small companies); style of creating stakeholder relations in investment areas and relating to possible resistance [such as underestimating resistance potential (CD1) or using sophisticated corporate countertactics to curb mobilization (CD3)]; the specific type of third party linked to the proposed project [such as tourism, agriculture, or another significant mining-critical industry (T1)]; and ore going primarily to China (T2).

I will first assess the role of foreign governments, with specific notes on whether trade with China (T2) surfaced as a delimiting factor in resistance success. After this, I study the role of united and dispersed capital on investment outcomes. Then, I assess whether it matters if the target of resistance is a public or private company or a large or small one. Last, the causal influence of two variations of corporate reactions to resistance are assessed: Resistance underestimation and curbing of mobilization by CSR, Social License to Operate (SLO), public-private partnerships (PPPs), and other sophisticated corporate agency tools. These factors help to show how there are many forms of corporate agency, with important variations across places. The QCA was used to shed light on whether or not these factors played a key role in influencing the outcomes of investment politics instead of other factors, such as resistance strategies. Next, this analysis is deepened further, on the basis of the QCA findings, to show how broader theoretical points can be made via and following QCA.

Third parties and international relations

Movement outcomes literature has emphasized that third parties must be studied in order to understand outcomes (Luders 2010). Foreign powers, particularly global hegemons or rising powers, have been the most important third parties in local conflicts crucial to the expansion of global capitalism (particularly via extractivism) for at least the last five centuries (Arrighi 1994; Moore 2015; Wallerstein 1974) and most likely much longer.[10] China, as a rising giant and the largest new buyer of resources, perhaps has played the most important third-party role in resource conflicts since 2005. Given the political and economic contexts, we might expect that the situation of resistance against iron exports is harder in Brazil than in India. The Brazilian and Indian governments have very different diplomatic and trade relations with China, particularly in terms of mineral policy. The Brazilian government's policy is not to sell as much as it can to China, rather it is to balance the negative trade account resulting from the importation of cheap consumer goods for the new middle classes of Brazil without considering the strategic importance of iron ore or not caring due to its massive reserves. The Indian government, on the contrary, woke up to the reality that its limited reserves of strategic iron ore were being depleted quickly by illegal miners who were exporting to a historic and key rival, China, with whom they have had border clashes.

If a country depletes its own reserves and there is a war, iron ore is likely to immediately become a very strategic mineral, the (non)trade of which can be used as a weapon. China is currently quickly depleting its own reserves, which are of very low quality in global comparisons, especially in contrast to India and Brazil. India currently seems to have at least twice the amount of reserves as China when considering the average iron content (author's analysis based on the data in BNDES 2014). It is no wonder that China has been willing to pay a high price for iron ore over the past several years in order to amass a safe reserve. The absence of access to this mineral, even theoretically, is a serious obstacle to a would-be world power.

In 2013, Brazil exported 173 mt of iron to China, which is more than the whole national production of India. In a decade, Brazil's exports to China have increased 4.5-fold.[11] This situates China as a crucial boom driver and a key third party to the resistance targeting Brazilian iron ore producers. For the Brazilian resistance, targeting of the iron ore production in Brazil is a much more difficult task than in India for a number of reasons, including the scale of exports, production, and the relative importance of iron ore in Brazilian exports. There are very few accessible global alternatives for China to achieve such massive iron ore imports besides Brazil; in fact, Australia has been one of the few available options and that is where most production has gone after exports have waned in India and expansion has been halted in Brazil. India, for example, is no longer a contender, because the country has banned increases in the export of minerals to China or elsewhere, retaining them for local steel plants. This signifies that resistance in India has rarely had to face such a powerful third party as that posed by a national government-China trade nexus. In this sense, the court's decision to cancel iron ore licenses in Goa, which primarily exported its production to China, was in line with Indian government policy to curb exports of key minerals, particularly to China. Therefore, the resistance successes in India have to be understood in the broader geopolitical setting, where countries have differing national coalitions that influence resource extraction and trade decisions (see Solingen and Gourevitch 2017). Wanting to counter China's rise, the Indian government has created Memoranda of Understanding (MOUs) with other global powers.[12] Brazil has, since the election of Bolsonaro, moved away from pursuing a multipolar world order and cast itself as a close partner to Trump's United States (in subservience, in a vassal-like relationship disguised as strong nationalist rhetoric). The curbing of iron exports from India, in combination with the failure to expand iron extraction in the forecasted manner in Brazil, has meant that China has had to search for new sources for its iron appetite since the mid-2010s. They have found a solution through the booming import of iron ore from Australia (Kröger 2019). However, this has created new vulnerabilities for China, as Australia is aligned with the United States' geopolitical strategies. In this sense, the resistance in India and Brazil at the points of production, in the big picture, has benefited Western global players at the cost of China, which has had to pay more for resources either monetarily or in terms of continuity and diplomatic trade-offs. This suggests that any study of extractivism has to consider the role of international trade and diplomacy. Yet, international relations that do not analyze the local, regional, and national scales cannot explain the major regional variations across countries.

A setting of competing corporate agencies within the same place or polity can help the resistance. In Brazil, the state and industrial elites, both national and foreign, are quite united and have a "capitalism of ties" (Kröger 2012; Lazzarini 2011), whereas in India there seem to be more conflicts between large or ethnically national (though officially multinational) mining capitalists, state capitalists, and foreign companies. Reserves are more limited in India than in Brazil, which might explain the greater intercapitalist struggles.[13] For the resistance, intercapitalist competition in India seems to present more of an opportunity than the united front of capital present in Brazil.

I recommend using this kind of incorporated comparison as a method of analysis and description when one wants to add an international relations (IR) dimension to QCA. The preceding analysis of IR and complex interactions between corporations, different nation-states, and evolving global dynamics is a type of input that should be included to supplement QCA in order to ensure that these types of complex international interactions are also covered. Next, I will provide details about what aspects of corporate agency need to be considered when investment politics are assessed. As in the previous section, I will detail how this can be done in practice.

Corporate agency and the state

How is corporate agency, including corporate strategies and composition, related to resistance outcomes? To delve into several aspects of this question, I have included fully state-owned, fully private, and mixed corporate structures in my data set, as well as quite varied corporate strategies that were used in the struggles. I will briefly discuss whether and how state ownership, company size, and corporate-agency style might most influence the causal path, from resistance efforts to outcomes.

My key method has been to look at the issue studied from as many viewpoints as possible to arrive at a comprehensive understanding of a phenomenon, through a thorough intellectual process. Therefore, I made several inquiries for my broad data set based on reviews of the existing mining, social movement, and Indian and Brazilian social scientific literatures and based on the many factors reported by the persons I interviewed to be able to explain how and why mining has or has not been discontinued. I then refined the questions to the factors analyzed in the QCA chapter, on the basis of the original basic questions found either in the literature or in the field. One question that arose from prior research, without solid answers, was the following: Are public mines an easier target for resistance than private ones? My data show that this question is either too simplistic or phrased incorrectly, as there are no clear answers. One activist argued that it is easier to target a public mine, such as Kudremukh, as the public mining company had less money than the private sector to bribe state officials and politicians. He added that, in general, it is easier to fight public money rather than private, backing his claim with a long list of litigations he had brought. In Kudremukh, there was only one target, the state, which owned the mine. He argued that the governments in eastern India have made alliances with multinational and private capital; thus, it is harder to resist these projects. The resistance has, in his view, been stronger in the East but has had comparatively fewer notable outcomes. Yet, in my database, there were countless public mines that were not closed in India. Clearly, the public-private divide cannot explain the situation.

What seemed to be more important is the quality of state support that the capital is enjoying, regardless of the type. As corporate agency and capitalism are so dependent on the state to be able to function—this is particularly true when land and resource control need to be secured—it makes sense that the kind of state and state relations in which the capital operates make more of a difference when explaining investment outcomes than the quality of the capital per se. When the state does not have a monopoly of violence, as in the Maoist revolutionary and secessionist strongholds of eastern India, there are competing claims to statehood. For example, the Naxalite-Maoist attacks, which targeted practically all private and multinational capital, but not all public capital, resulted from a particular Naxal-mining capital relation. In this relation, the Naxals questioned the right of the Indian states to form alliances with private national or multinational capital or to expand through state-owned companies in forest areas inhabited by Adivasis and considered to be strategically important for the armed revolutionary actors. Some state-owned companies' mines were left in peace, if their operation or quality was considered to be of appropriate socialist quality by the Maoists, while other state-capital relations were questioned through armed resistance. This kind of state-capital relation should be considered as competing with the state relations of private national and multinational capital.

For the thrust of corporate agency, it makes a difference whether one is talking about large, multinational mining companies or small, local operators. A key factor is the difference in the availability of funds for these two. Between 2002 and 2011, Vale's total shareholder return at 31.8% was the highest in the world. For Vale's biggest rivals, the respective figures were as follows: BHP Billiton 23.8%, Rio Tinto 14.4%, and Anglo American 10.8% (Bloomberg, cited in Vale 2012). These four companies are mining behemoths, and it is plausible to assume that resistance attempts against them have a lower chance of success, as these companies have more resources to counterattack than the smaller players. Their high and stable profit rates ensure a continued corporate agency. When comparing the outcomes of struggles as divided into conflicts targeting small- or medium-sized companies and conflicts targeting these large companies, it is clear that a more typical outcome in large-company conflicts (CD2 = 1) was changing the extraction style, while in small-company conflicts (CD2 = 0) a more likely outcome was curbing the pace of extraction. However, there were also cases where the projects of large companies were halted, such as Vale's Apolo project, but this was a greenfield project. The large-scale closures of running mine operations in my database did not affect the largest global mining multinationals. Özkaynak et al. (2015, 45) observed a similar type of correlation when environmental justice activists were interviewed about how they perceived their success in mining struggles. When the target was a key global mining company, it was much more likely that the answer given by activists was they were "not sure if there was success," rather than "success" or "no success."

There are varied reasons for this discrepancy. Large companies may prefer to change their extraction style in order to support continued production rather than deepen conflicts. The more sophisticated corporate agency of many mining multinationals, including dialogues and perks to counter resistance, is more attuned to finding the least costly option to curb a conflict—typically a change in extraction style. They know better than the small companies how to sell this to locals as a "solution."[14] Conversely, the inability of smaller companies to understand the importance of their corporate agency and reactiveness to resistance demands is more likely to lead to a complete closure of operations rather than to a change in the extraction style or just taking a hard line. As problems compound and the anger of people is not addressed, the resistance has time to find new strategies, such as embedding the state, protesting, and campaigning, thus leading to more profound results from the movement viewpoint.

Until the 2000s, most Indian mining was conducted by a few, very large, national enterprises, with state companies as the biggest extractors. The iron ore boom of the 2000s, however, changed this dynamic. Those places that had dormant leases dating as far back as the Second World War era were activated; this includes sites in Goa and Odisha.[15] New operators started small-scale mines as greenfield operations, often lacking environmental licenses and overstepping lease boundaries. While these small, rampant mines could be seen as "easier" targets than large established ones, there are many obvious objections to such size-based claims (e.g., Kudremukh and a wide range of quite old, large mines closed following the Shah Commission's work). It is clear that company size itself does not cause the difference, but corporate agency style does, which may or may not follow the pathways described previously when responding to resistance. The dynamics of contention between such agencies and complex causalities are not self-explanatory through a mere QCA truth table observation; the causal relations between QCA factors need to be revealed for their complexity and relations through the kind of explanatory analysis provided herein as an example. Comparison between cases is also key here.

Several activists argued that it is crucial to look at corporate counterstrategies to understand how and when resistance succeeds or fails. With the surge of CSR, SLO, and deeper stakeholder relations [such as the Towards Sustainable Mining program (TSM) in Canada and its extension in Finland], the mining industry and many corporations are becoming increasingly complex entities that do not just try to directly maximize profits without consideration for the resistance but try to actively shape the political landscape in which they are located (see Bebbington and Bury 2013; Kirsch 2013; Li 2015;

Rajak 2011). These attempts range from spying on resistance movements and co-optation attempts to dialogue and playing the role of middleman to help movements get what they want in their other struggles. Vale has been accused of doing all of these things (Zhouri and Valencio 2014). In fact, the last of these, the middleman role, was something that the directors of the Vale Foundation, whom I interviewed, brought to my attention. Vale, and particularly the Vale Foundation in Brazil, has started to act as a type of NGO middleman between the locals and the state, offering assistance to municipalities in approaching the central state and to movements in their social-benefit advocacy vis-à-vis the state. In July 2014, a Vale Foundation director said the following to me in an interview (translated by the author from Portuguese):

> Municipalities do not know how to do planning, for example for sanitation. We contract engineers for municipalities, and also offer for example didactic material for municipal schools [on behalf of the state]. We also help in professionalization, to create more capable public officers, as there is a lack of resources to professionalize them. Today the state also has money and resources, and also public policies, but municipalities do not know how to apply for these or how to use them well. Vale Foundation helps them to get these and implement the resources well. We function thus as an auxiliary entity, in these public-private partnerships (PPPs). PPPs are the way to take what is best in society, state or companies to improve the local quality of life. For example, the people do not have access to municipal governments, but they have Vale: they want it to open the channel.

In this way, Vale became well-connected with myriad local governments and communities, offering them help to obtain resources from elsewhere—this is indeed quite an important aspect to explain why, in many cases in Brazil, mining has not been resisted as much as in other parts of Latin America or India. The locals are tied into relations of favors to be reciprocated.[16] The four largest iron ore mines in the world are in Brazil, and all are owned by Vale (one, the infamous Samarco, whose tailings pond dam ruptured in November 2015 in Mariana, the Bento Rodrigues dam catastrophe, is half-owned by BHB). My comprehensive database shows that these have not been as uniformly and/or strongly resisted by locals as the greenfield or small-operator iron mines. Vale's corporate agency has made a big difference in keeping existing mining operations running by diverting potential resistance (as Vale's successful reaction to Samarco's Tsulama, a rupture that created a tsunami of mud, also demonstrates).[17] I did not notice that companies in India had such strategic corporate outreach plans to position themselves in a key role in the flow of public resources and trust.

However, other corporate tools to curb mobilization do exist in India. In Odisha, an activist observed that companies systematically use strategies to disorganize and depoliticize local people:

> How to break unity is a key goal and method of companies. [In one case] a community leader taking money sold lies to tribals in their own language. The tribals believed blindly in their community leader. After this the unity [of the local people resisting] was broken.

This tactic was prevalent across eastern India, and in Chhattisgarh's Bastar region this sowing of disunity has gone so far as to foster a civil war. In Brazil, movements have mostly shielded themselves from this device by ensuring autonomy, but in some places the local population continues to be divided, for example, through CSR perks and personal meetings that make it difficult to mobilize people in a culture with deep roots in clientelism and personal friendships (see Kröger 2013).

Parallel to the preceding strengths and qualities of corporate agency, the underestimation of resistance potential by the targets (CD1) surfaced as a factor that must be considered in order to understand causal complexes. The elites in Goa completely underestimated the power of the resistance they faced and its ability to halt mining (several interviews, 2010–2013). This underestimation was potentially one of the most important factors that allowed the movements to build a strong case to bring to the courts by documenting mining illegalities. In Carajás, on the other hand, Vale takes the resistance movements very seriously, particularly the MST and indigenous groups, and has hired anthropologists to help them with risk assessment. Nonetheless, the potential of NGO resistance in pro-mining Minas Gerais was underestimated by Vale in some of its projects in 2012–2013. In 2014, however, companies had learned from their past mistakes and the dynamics of resistance underestimation, which made the situation all the more complex for movements. It seems to be the case that when targets underestimate resistance potential, better results can be expected [Luders (2010) found the same]. Yet, comparison of this to other causal conditions indicates that it is not a necessary condition for achieving important results. In eastern India, the elites and their companies[18] also take the resistance very seriously due to the area being largely under Naxalite control. These and other corporate agency factors should be discussed in much more detail, particularly in studies of extractive capitalism.

I have detailed here the theory and complexities behind several of the QCA factors that were assessed systematically in Chapter 3. QCA was used to systematically compare the impacts and causal condition complexes formed by the contingency factors, such as CD1–CD3, discussed in this chapter. In order to analyze so many factors across so many cases in a coherent and comprehensible manner, a systematic methodology is needed, including tools such as the QCA truth tables. Otherwise, it becomes increasingly difficult to keep all the factors and their complex causal conditions in mind and to identify their relations to outcomes. Therefore, the causal analysis is best done by uniting these different factors instead of assessing them separately. The interrelation of these causal conditions emerged as a key feature that often explained more than just the presence or absence of this or that factor. This chapter assessed several important contextual and contingency factors separately to provide more detail on how each of the factors in the QCA truth tables was analyzed, and the final chapter draws some overarching conclusions.

Notes

1 Oxum is one of the principal divinities in the Afro-Brazilian Umbanda and other religions. She helps and guides humanity to live on this planet. She also takes human form, for example, breastfeeding a baby by a riverside, which represents all of her beauty and kindness (her sources of power). She reigns especially over freshwater. Here are two pictorial representations of Oxum, one in the form of a river and the other as a woman: https://upload.wikimedia.org/wikipedia/commons/1/17/Rio_Osun.jpg and https://upload.wikimedia.org/wikipedia/commons/9/90/Oxum_Ekodide.jpg.
2 In September 2020, NACAB won an important victory as judges decided in its favor against the interests of the corporate-state nexus to expand tailings ponds. https://londonminingnetwork.org/2020/09/legal-victory-over-anglo-american-in-brazil/ (accessed November 13, 2020).
3 By ethnicity, I refer to caste, race, indigeneity, traditionality, genes, and/or constructed ethnic-territorial identities or any combination of these factors. Class is an economic category that may or may not correlate with, and be causally related to, the construction of ethnicity and interethnic relations. In detailed ethnographic research, intersectional analysis should be conducted in consideration of the interplay of gender, ethnicity, and class. QCA can be used to identify some key causal factors related to ethnicity. In my research, these surfaced as an essential factor in understanding both the pushing and resisting aspects of investment politics.
4 These rural populations have been cast as outsiders in Brazil's new global positioning, where the country provides resources taken from the these groups—at any cost, including violence against resistance—primarily to China in exchange for consumer goods (mostly not for the rural poor), making the Brazil-China connection the most significant global-level cause of the iron ore boom and concomitant conflicts (Moreno 2015).
5 According to Kakar and Kakar (2007, 154),

> Communalism is a specifically Indian concept which signifies a strong identification with a community of believers based not only on religion but also common social, political and especially economic interests which conflict with the corresponding interests of another community of believers—the "enemy"—sharing the same geographic space.

This type of definition that does not mention caste applies more to the north of India, whereas in the South, communalism more often takes the form of caste groups (Wilkinson 2013).

6 However, Baverstock (n.d., 69–70) notes that the Adivasi villagers in the Thakurani Reserve Forest of Joda, about 1,000 people, face dire pollution from the established mines and are being violently displaced by mine expansions, which they greatly resent and "protest" against. Baverstock does not describe what is meant by "protesting," though as I heard no other accounts of visible, mass-scale mobilizations, I consider the use of this word to refer more to a voiced objection than the use of large-scale marches and organized effort. In general, the Adivasis in Joda have responded by fleeing the expansion, not resisting openly, a dynamic that is very different from Banspal and other Keonjhar blocks. However, these observations should be confirmed by detailed field research.

7 According to HNF (June 29, 2007), a key factor to understand the failure to build a strong resistance organization in Joda was ethnic cleavage within the budding movement, wherein the leaders were not from the same ethnic background,

> Even the leaders of these tribals who, unfortunately, happen to be non-tribal people are all using the suffering tribals for their own benefit. As the whispering on the local and the district administrative corridors goes, some noted leaders are instigating the tribals to get a contract filling 50–100 rags of ores. Virtually nobody works for the welfare of these tribal communities, which are suffering from the cumulative impact of pollution, corruption, and administrative apathy.

http://hotnhitnews.com/joda-barbil_mining_hub_a_death_trap.htm (accessed August 3, 2015).

8 World-systems scholars such as Wallerstein (1998) as well as ecofeminists (Mies and Shiva 2014) have argued that creating ruptures among potential resistance movements (particularly workers) along racial, ethnic, gender, and other sociocultural lines has been key to quelling the organization of mass power against global capitalism.

9 Both religious intolerance and attacks on indigenous people have been on the rise due to the fanaticism and extremism epitomized by the political rise of President Jair Bolsonaro, a topic beyond the scope of analysis herein as I focus primarily on the period before 2015.

10 Foreign powers and the world system may have been the key forces of change (also in global mining) for 5,000 years. Frank and Gills (1993) argue that capital imperialism has been present since the Bronze Age, with wealthy families and state power being the oscillating key driving forces of this expansion. There is still a need to study the past 5,000 years of mining politics, including possible resistance, from this world-systems perspective.

11 http://usa.chinadaily.com.cn/world/2014-01/27/content_17259987.htm (accessed July 10, 2015).

12 For example, it vehemently supported the South Korean–Western-capital-based POSCO company project in Odisha—in which it nevertheless failed. This is mostly due to very strong local resistance, whose struggle has been eased as there have been other third parties, including national capitalists, that are also against POSCO.

13 POSCO is in conflict both with state-owned Indian mining companies and with Tata, which would like to displace POSCO and instead locate its own steel

project in the same area or close by, taking over the potential captive mine, according to an Odishan researcher I interviewed. He claimed that POSCO, however, has more power than Tata, as the politicians want to lure in multinationals because they can thus create more "black money." Furthermore, local politicians receive much more pressure from the Centre (the Indian central government), as a result of South Korean diplomacy. The Centre could use its support for the project as a bargaining chip for other perks in other areas of trade, diplomacy, and international relations from South Korea and other countries whose citizens and companies own shares in POSCO and/or would get the steel and the ore. POSCO's appearance on the scene has also meant that not only Tata but also other steel companies, such as Mittal, have been unable to put pressure on the Centre (according to a Tehelka journalist following the issue), as Odisha was already marked for POSCO in the higher levels of diplomacy.

14 For a prominent example, in my interviews in Canada in 2013, several Canadian mining activists and trade unionists argued that Canada's TSM program functions as a tool that quells protests by arguing that extraction style will be improved via stakeholder dialogues and voluntary actions within the industry [for a discussion of the TSM, see Fitzpatrick, Fonseca, and McAllister (2011)].

15 In the 1940s, Britain had distributed low-cost leases to upper-caste speculative investors in the hope of receiving a supply of crucial minerals from its colony. Wars are important episodes shaping global commodity networks, even dormant ones. Decisions made during World War II were acutely materialized with the rise of China in the 2000s.

16 This kind of dynamics is omnipresent in Brazil's political economy of big corporations (Kröger 2012), which is the reason Lazzarini (2011) calls the Brazilian variety of capitalism a "capitalism of ties."

17 See the analysis of how Vale managed to shed its responsibility by Marcos Pedlowski, for example, https://blogdopedlowski.com/2016/01/25/tsulama-da-samarco-governo-dilma-fecha-acordo-do-raposa-tomando-conta-do-galinheiro-com-mineradoras/ (accessed March 31, 2016). See also Zonta and Trocate (2016).

18 Elites include, for example, the Mittal family of ArcelorMittal, the world's largest steel company originating in India and with a business plan based on "grabbing" privatized steel mills at low prices (see Cock, Lambert, and Fitzgerald 2013) and acquiring more areas in eastern India.

Conclusions

Chapter Abstract: *This concluding chapter summarizes the contribution of this methodological book, which showcases, through a practical study, how data collected primarily via multi-sited political ethnography, supplemented by other materials, and verified by multiple forms of triangulation can be systematically analyzed through QCA. This book presents findings from a large research project that compared the political dynamics across all of the major iron ore mining areas and projects in Brazil and India between 2000 and 2015. The results of this QCA and further elaboration of the "behind-the-scenes" reasoning for the choices made during the QCA show how to study the political and economic outcomes in natural resource conflicts across different contexts and political systems. I call this approach to analyzing natural resource conflict through QCA the study of investment politics, which broadens the scope of social movement studies.*

Methodological lessons

In this book, I have laid out what should be taken into account when designing this kind of research approach and strategy, including where to start and how to proceed. I have also discussed potential pitfalls and how to resolve them. There is a detailed discussion, which utilized practical examples from my own research, on how to further ensure data integrity and suitable approaches to data verification.

This book has shown how to utilize specific methods to make sense of complex databases through systematic comparisons. I showed how QCA can be applied in practice to find sufficient and necessary configurations of causal conditions that lead to outcomes. This book helped to expand QCA to new disciplinary arenas beyond political science and sociology, which has been demanded in the literature (Fiss, Marx, and Rihoux 2014; Rihoux et al. 2009). The wider disciplinary use of this method combined with an increase in transdisciplinary approaches has opened up new methodological possibilities.

Existing debates on QCA were addressed, and new methodological points were made, on the basis of a test of the method across many more causal conditions than is usual in QCA. I have found, in line with others in the field (e.g., Baumgartner and Thiem 2020; Ragin 2014; Rihoux 2020), that QCA is still viable and useful despite critique. There is still space for further development and discussion concerning the ways in which QCA can be used. My focus was on offering a simpler form of QCA application, as recommended by Collier (2014), for example. As QCA software programs and data sets used in increasingly complex mathematical elaborations have proliferated, the original intention of Ragin to use QCA for case-oriented research in a reflexive way, and never in a "push-button" manner, has been partly lost. There is thus a need to take a step back from a mechanical approach (Rihoux and Ragin 2009, 173). I have showed here how to conduct multiple, back and forth iterations between case-based information and QCA: This is a requirement for QCA through its application as a case-oriented method (Rihoux and Lobe 2009).

The debate around what QCA should be used for has recently oscillated between the argument that QCA serves primarily for finding causally relevant conditions (Baumgartner and Thiem 2020) and the argument for a continued, yet adjusted, focus on seeking parsimonious explanations (Dușa 2019). I made observations based on my QCA application similar to those of Dușa (2019), who criticized the search for parsimonious solutions and suggested instead that conservative solutions work better to reveal causal paths, as these are based on actually observing the causal chains, than the logistical algorithms used in parsimony-seeking. "Conservative solutions" are actually the most "liberal," as they are not as strict in pointing out which configurations are causally relevant as QCA's parsimonious search strategy (Baumgartner and Thiem 2020). The latest research on QCA solution types (parsimonious, conservative, or intermediate) (Haesebrouck and Thomann 2021) supports these claims that focusing on conservative solutions is the appropriate way to uncover causal mechanisms (Álamos-Concha et al. 2021). In this book, I recommended that one should not include logical remainders when engaged in comparative analysis of ethnography-based comparative case studies, which would be impossible, but instead one should only include those configurations and outcomes that have actually occurred. A similar critique has been voiced against the algorithmic and technical use of QCA by Collier (2014), for example. However, instead of completely shying away from existing QCA tools, I also showed how—through the use of the excellent Excel QCA add-in developed by Cronqvist (2019)—these can be used to cross-check and identify contradictory configurations and to work more deeply with the data, thus returning to the data set with new observations. However, as Dușa (2019) points out, the parsimonious solutions offered by QCA software and logic cannot be trusted automatically, as they can produce insufficient and even incorrect accounts. Instead, impossible configurations should be excluded from the process of minimization, an approach Duşa calls an "intermediate solution." This book has shown, by utilizing practice-based examples, how this kind of approach is more suitable in QCA applications. However, if one does not know the empirical data well but uses QCA for predominately secondary source data, then the suggestion by Baumgartner and Thiem (2020) to favor a parsimonious search strategy instead of intermediate solutions might be warranted. There are different uses for QCA, depending on the type of data used, and this book has shown different ways in which QCA helped to work through complex data sets and causalities. This application of QCA has the potential to yield insights on causalities that would have been hard to observe without this kind of systematic technique; perhaps such observations would even be impossible. The key methodological takeaway from this rare book on QCA (as the data are based on material collected primarily via multi-sited political ethnography) is a reiteration of the suggestion by prior QCA developers, such as Olsen (2014, 105), that methods, debates, and tests utilized should "make reference to the real world, not to purely numerical patterns." The roles of theory and societal complexity need to be further embraced in methodological discussions and guides. QCA is most often used to evaluate theory (Rihoux 2020). Herein, Chapter 3 showed how one can make theoretical observations and claims via QCA, while Chapter 4 illustrated how to write about these QCA results and expand them further.

Lessons on applying QCA to complex ethnographic data

This book has offered a practical, hands-on guide for how to apply QCA to study complex causalities and their outcomes. It explored a particular research project, offering an example of the methodological choices that a scholar needs to make. In this chapter, I recap some of the key steps included in this process through reflection on my own methodological path. It is important for QCA users to be transparent about their research documentation and decision-making throughout the analysis process. This level of transparency also allows for reflexivity.

The field research for this specific project started in 2010. It was after I finished a doctorate in world politics, where my dissertation focused on industrial forestry in Latin America and the impacts of resistance on its expansion (Kröger 2010). In my dissertation, I identified five resistance strategies that I applied across all Brazilian pulp investment cases to explain tree plantation expansion outcomes. In 2010, when I began this new project, my initial broad hypothesis was that this set of five resistance strategies could explain resistance outcomes more generally. I wanted to explore whether these strategies could also explain other resource conflicts and politics beyond Latin America and forestry, that is, in differing contingencies, contexts, and extractive sectors. I studied over 20 mining cases in different contexts and polities in detail to test this hypothesis. I wanted to test the limits of QCA methodology, observing not only a maximum of five to seven causal conditions but over 20 causal conditions across all 20-plus cases.

The main finding of this testing was that one can use QCA to make analyses across a wide variety of causal conditions and outcomes. However, if one does take on this type of complex analysis, it is best to utilize the following methodological tactics.

1. Break the conditions into different subsets and study these separately and as possibly competing and complementary explanatory sets.
2. Make a probabilistic analysis, instead of seeking a minimal formula, to explain how probable it was for a given causal condition to be of importance in explaining a given outcome. For example, write that, "causal condition x was active in 20 of the 23 cases with the outcome y," and then explain what the three discrepant cases signify. Contextual explanations can be used to better understand when the anomaly configurations occur. These explanations should be based on deeper ethnographic research, field research, or other material.
3. There are facets of the research process wherein one should search for the minimal formula, especially to find contradictory configurations, by cross-examinations of subsets of conditions with differing outcomes. This allows one to make full use of the broader database and to spot causalities, problems, and interesting dynamics from the database that would be very difficult to spot without using a systematic tool like QCA.
4. The minimal formula exercise can then be used to proceed to a more formal and typical QCA application by selecting the five to seven key causal conditions and the most interesting outcome for closer examination. In this process the cases are revisited, and less important or problematic cases may be removed in support of pursuing a parsimonious explanation. However, any removal should be carefully justified. After this, the overall database should be revisited with fresh insights from the more limited comparisons.
5. As a word of advice, one should not extend and create causal conditions too lightly or expand a research project to such a wide scope that the whole becomes very difficult to comprehend, manage, and write about. Therefore, although two-country and cross-contextual comparisons are useful in many senses, such as highlighting crucial polity

and contextual differences, I would recommend trying to keep the key contextual parameters fixed. In practical terms, I would recommend starting with the observation of only one state in a country that is as large as Brazil or India, and only then proceeding to the national level. Until one is more comfortable with the method, it is best to avoid making cross-country comparisons. That analytical process requires intense effort, and it would be easier to do first one country and only then another one. One can even break up the countries, or other entities on which the research is focused, into smaller units of analysis. This is an especially pertinent piece of advice if one is just starting a master's, PhD, or postdoctoral project. The results of these more focused studies can be published as short journal articles. Once one is comfortable with the method and the research context, QCA can be used for more complex comparisons.

I chose to focus on csQCA, which is the simplest form of QCA and has thus far been criticized by some scholars as being too crude of a tool. However, quantitative analysis would be just as arbitrary as the Boolean logic of csQCA and mvQCA, because instead one can use the strategy of identifying new or specifying more precise causal conditions. For example, in social movement studies, the indication that a resistance group's use of the "protesting" strategy in a particular case had a strength of 59 or 78 out of 100 would be less precise than specifying the number of protests of a particular quality, that is, how one would approach the analysis with mvQCA. However, csQCA and mvQCA (and simple forms of fsQCA having, for example, four-value fuzzy sets based on qualitative assessments) are useful tools for exploring investment politics and social movements in the dynamics of contention perspective. For example, in some of my work on the forestry industry (Kröger 2011, 2013) I found, through the use of csQCA and mvQCA, that what mattered for the outcome was not the use of just any kind of protesting but specifically pioneering, nonviolent, massive (over 300 people), mass-media-noted, disruptive, and resymbolizing protesting. These protests took the form of land occupation, roadblocks, marches, or other protest acts, where novelty and innovation were central to achieving the desired outcome. I arrived at this finding after multiple rounds of mvQCA, intermeshed with multi-sited political ethnography, whereby the new cases (which resulted in a database with no nonobserved cases—in other words, all Brazilian pulp investments were observed) offered new ideas on the generalizable strategy for which the causal condition value 1 (active) with the mvQCA value of 3 or 4 (number of qualifying protests), for example, could be given. QCA can be used to detect the pathways that social movements can use to influence outcomes.

When starting field visits, I did not yet have much knowledge about the cases, the outcomes, or all the potential causal conditions. The field research allowed me to amass this knowledge as I progressed through my project. One of the first steps in my research process was to map all of the major iron mining projects in Brazil and India. Then, in conjunction with an extensive literature and secondary-document review, I used the snowball method to conduct interviews and visit important field sites. The primary methodology I employed during the field research was to provide an open space for informants to share their experiences and views on mining politics for the cases they knew. I typically walked with the informant at the sites of conflict and mining expansion or conducted interviews in their premises, if field-site-based interviews were not possible. During these discussions, new categories of potential causalities and dynamics were introduced organically by my informants. I created a code for each new category and then looked at my other cases to see whether these causalities and dynamics were also present. In addition to the more open-ended discussions, I also utilized semistructured interviews to delve more deliberately into specific questions. These interviews mostly revolved around whether the strategies that were central in movement scholarship were also used in practice by my informants in their respective cases.

When the data were collected, my scrutiny of possible resistance impacts started from observing cases where project expansion had been slowed by resistance groups. I then worked through all the possible explanations for this outcome and discarded the explanations that did not fit. What was left can be considered the configuration of necessary causal conditions that led to the specific result. I systematically compared the cases where one of the following paths was taken by local people: (1) The resistance had mobilized new, important movements focused on the mining; (2) they had done something else, for example, supported mining continuation; or (3) they had not been active in a specific political direction. This comparison was performed in order to highlight causal condition complexes and used QCA methodology as a tool of systematic inquiry. In addition to the cases where the resistance had an impact, I also studied cases where they did not have an impact. In these cases, the resistance had made only a small difference in the mining trajectories or made no impact on the expansions. These comparisons across the variations in the dependent variable were instrumental in allowing the utilization of QCA to establish the sufficient causal conditions.

QCA was used to illustrate how one can empirically study complex settings and causalities, such as how the flow of globally crucial commodities, like iron ore and steel, can be influenced. Utilization of the QCA minimal formula and probabilistic analysis uncovered the most important strategies for resistance to attain its goal, which in my analysis were protests and avoidance of private negotiations. Use of the method also showed that, although these strategies were necessary in all of the discontinuation cases, they were not as sufficient on their own as other resistance strategies, and many other contextual and contingency factors played a role. In this probabilistic approach, what mattered more than finding exact solutions was finding how likely it was for different types of causal condition complexes to result in differing types of outcomes. QCA made this approach possible, and this is recommended as one type of application for the technique (Ragin 1987, 2014).

QCA should be followed by drawing broader theoretical lessons on the topics at stake. In the examples used in this book, social movement scholarship was advanced methodologically. In addition, some theoretical findings on causalities can also be drawn from this analysis. Bosi, Giugni, and Uba (2016), Amenta et al. (2010), and others have called for more research on movement outcomes, and my comparison here provides some answers on the causalities leading to outcomes in the iron ore mining sectors in Brazil and India.

As described earlier in detail, my findings illustrate that the five key resistance strategies (a–e) play an important role, particularly in some sectors and contexts, although their causal relation to outcomes cannot be generalized across all contexts and sectors. The setting and testing of the hypothesis—that is, that this specific set of resistance strategies can generally explain investment outcomes across sectors, despite the contingencies and contexts—were helpful, as they led me to explore all of these issues in detail.

I also discussed the constraints of QCA, especially when used together with ethnographic data. The obvious constraint in csQCA is the Boolean logic used to mark a causal condition as either active (1) or nonactive (0) in a given case. This base judgment of whether a condition is active or inactive should be supplemented by the depiction of political ethnographic observations and contextual and relational analyses based on interviews, statistics, and other materials. I provided a detailed example of how this should be done by assessing the role of ethnic relations and corporate agency and by writing specific subchapters on these more complex topics, following the QCA truth table analysis. An example of a finding from this deeper analysis of ethnic relations was that the underlying metacultural differences, which shape how cultural differences are organized within a given context, seemed to be an important factor in resistance. This finding and other findings like these are useful because they can be examined further in future studies.

This book has showed how to use QCA to analyze data collected through the observation of over 20 cases. When one collects a large database with dozens of recorded interviews and extensive field notes, they have to be systematically analyzed. QCA is an excellent tool for making the findings and analysis more understandable and readable; indeed, it has been understood as a way to organize data. However, it is a tool that anthropologists, ethnographers, and others conducting field-research-based studies could use much more, not only to organize their data across the settings they study but to analyze commonalities and discrepancies and to go beyond mere localized or case studies. My application of this research methodology and strategy to explain the complexities of the world has served to strengthen the point made by Ragin (2019): Case studies based on a small- or medium-n data set are not inferior to large-n studies but can in fact provide very deep insights and theories. Hopefully, the practice-based examples herein of how one can organize, execute, and present the analysis for a project utilizing QCA will help to demystify some of the more nuanced aspects of this powerful method.

References

Aarts, Kees. 2007. "Parsimonious Methodology." *Methodological Innovations Online* 2 (1): 2–10. https://doi.org/10.4256/mio.2007.0002

Álamos-Concha, Priscilla, Valérie Pattyn, Benoît Rihoux, Benjamin Schalembier, Derek Beach, and Bart Cambré. 2021, forthcoming. "On the Appropriateness of Different Solution Types When Combining Qualitative Comparative Analysis (QCA) and Process Tracing." *Quality and Quantity*.

Amenta, Edwin, Neal Caren, Elizabeth Chiarello, and Yang Su. 2010. "The Political Consequences of Social Movements." *Annual Review of Sociology* 36: 287–307. https://doi.org/10.1146/annurev-soc-070308-120029

Arce, Moisés. 2014. *Resource Extraction and Protest in Peru*. Pittsburg, PA: University of Pittsburgh Press. https://doi.org/10.2307/j.ctt9qh8z9

Arrighi, Giovanni. 1994. *The Long Twentieth Century: Money, Power, and the Origins of Our Times*. London: Verso Books.

Arsel, Murat, Barbara Hogenboom, and Lorenzo Pellegrini. 2016. "The Extractive Imperative and the Boom in Environmental Conflicts at the End of the Progressive Cycle in Latin America." *The Extractive Industries and Society* 3: 877–879. https://doi.org/10.1016/j.exis.2016.10.013

Auyero, Javier. 2007. *Routine Politics and Violence in Argentina: The Gray Zone of State Power*. Cambridge: Cambridge University Press. https://doi.org/10.1017/CBO9780511814815

Auyero, Javier, and Débora Swistun. 2009. *Flammable: Environmental Suffering in an Argentine Shantytown*. New York: Oxford University Press.

Banerjee, Sumanta. 2013. "Radical and Violent Political Movements." In *Routledge Handbook of South Asian Politics*, edited by Paul R. Brass, 382–398. London: Routledge. https://doi.org/10.4324/9780203878187

Baumgartner, Michael, and Alrik Thiem. 2020. "Often Trusted But Never (Properly) Tested: Evaluating Qualitative Comparative Analysis." *Sociological Methods & Research* 49 (2): 279–311. https://doi.org/10.1177/0049124117701487

Baverstock, Philip. n.d. "The Price of Progress: Buying Development from the Poor." *Forum of Fact-Finding, Documentation and Advocacy (FFDA)*, Raipur, India.

Baviskar, Amita. 2001. "Written on the Body, Written on the Land: Violence and Environmental Struggles in Central India." In *Violent Environments*, edited by Nancy Peluso and Michael Watts, 354–379. Ithaca: Cornell University Press. https://doi.org/10.1177/1057567707302514

References

Beach, Derek, and Ramus Brun Pedersen. 2019. *Process-tracing Methods: Foundations and Guidelines.* Ann Arbor, MI: University of Michigan Press. https://doi.org/10.3998/mpub.10072208

Bebbington, Anthony, and Jeffrey Bury, eds. 2013. *Subterranean Struggles: New Dynamics of Mining, Oil, and Gas in Latin America.* Austin: University of Texas Press.

Berg-Schlosser, Dirk, Gisèle De Meur, Benoît Rihoux, and Charles Ragin. 2009. "Qualitative Comparative Analysis (QCA) as an Approach." In *Configurational Comparative Methods: Qualitative Comparative Analysis (QCA) and Related Techniques*, edited by Benoît Rihoux and Charles C. Ragin, 1–18. Thousand Oaks, CA: SAGE Publications. https://doi.org/10.4135/9781452226569

BNDES. 2014. "Minério de ferro. Insumos Básicos." Authors: Pedro Sergio Landim de Carvalho, Marcelo Machado da Silva, Marco Aurélio Ramalho Rocio and Jacques Moszkowicz. *BNDES Setorial* 39: 197–234.

Borras, Saturnino, and Jennifer Franco. 2013. "Global Land Grabbing and Political Reactions 'From Below'." *Third World Quarterly* 34 (9): 1723–1747. https://doi.org/10.1080/01436597.2013.843845

Bosi, Lorenzo, and Marco Giugni. 2012. "The Study of the Consequences of Armed Groups: Lessons from the Social Movement Literature." *Mobilization* 17 (1): 85–98. https://doi.org/10.17813/maiq.17.1.4k31637mquq41016

Bosi, Lorenzo, Marco Giugni, and Katrin Uba, eds. 2016. *The Consequences of Social Movements.* Cambridge: Cambridge University Press. https://doi.org/10.1017/CBO9781316337790

Bringel, Breno. 2019 "Latin American Perspectives on Social Movements Research." In *Key Texts for Latin American Sociology*, edited by Fernanda Beigel, 273–289. Los Angeles, CA: Sage.

Broad, Robin, and John Cavanagh. 2015. "Poorer Countries and the Environment: Friends or Foes?" *World Development* 72: 419–431. https://doi.org/10.1016/j.worlddev.2015.03.007

Brown, Cliff, and Terry Boswell. 1995. "Strikebreaking or Solidarity in the Great Steel Strike of 1919: A Split Labor Market, Game-Theoretic, and QCA Analysis." *American Journal of Sociology* 100 (6): 1479–1519. https://doi.org/10.1086/230669

Choudhary, Shubhranshu. 2012. *Let's Call Him Vasu: With the Maoists in Chhattisgarh.* New Delhi: Penguin.

Cock, Jacklyn, Rob Lambert, and Scott Fitzgerald. 2013. "Steel, Nature and Society." *Globalizations* 10 (6): 855–870. https://doi.org/10.1080/14747731.2013.814441

Collier, David. 2014. "Comment: QCA Should Set Aside the Algorithms." *Sociological Methodology* 44 (1): 122–126. https://doi.org/10.1177/0081175014542568

Conde, Marta. 2017. "Resistance to Mining. A Review." *Ecological Economics* 132: 80–90. https://doi.org/10.1016/j.ecolecon.2016.08.025

Cress, Daniel M., and David A. Snow. 2000. "The Outcomes of Homeless Mobilization: The Influence of Organization, Disruption, Political Mediation, and Framing." *American Journal of Sociology* 105 (4): 1063–1104. https://doi.org/10.1086/210399

Cronqvist, Lasse. 2019. *QCA Add-In* [Version 1.1]. University of Trier. www.qca-addin.net

References

Cronqvist, Lasse, and Dirk Berg-Schlosser. 2009. "Multi-value QCA (mvQCA)." In *Configurational Comparative Methods: Qualitative Comparative Analysis (QCA) and Related Techniques*, edited by Benoît Rihoux and Charles C. Ragin, 69–86. Thousand Oaks, CA: SAGE Publications, Inc. https://doi.org/10.4135/9781452226569.n4

de Block, Debora, and Barbara Vis. 2019. "Addressing the Challenges Related to Transforming Qualitative Into Quantitative Data in Qualitative Comparative Analysis." *Journal of Mixed Methods Research* 13 (4): 503–535. https://doi.org/10.1177/1558689818770061

De Meur, Gisèle, Benoît Rihoux, and Sakura Yamasaki. 2009. "Addressing the Critiques of QCA." In *Configurational Comparative Methods: Qualitative Comparative Analysis (QCA) and Related Techniques*, edited by Benoît Rihoux and Charles C. Ragin, 147–166. Thousand Oaks, CA: SAGE Publications, Inc. https://doi.org/10.4135/9781452226569.n7

De Pierris, Graciela, and Michael Friedman. 2018. "Kant and Hume on Causality." In *The Stanford Encyclopedia of Philosophy*, edited by Edward N. Zalta. https://plato.stanford.edu/archives/win2018/entries/kant-hume-causality/

Dougherty, Michael, and Tricia Olsen. 2014. "'They Have Good Devices': Trust, Mining, and the Microsociology of Environmental Decision-making." *Journal of Cleaner Production* 84: 183–192. https://doi.org/10.1016/j.jclepro.2014.04.052

Duşa, A. 2019. "Critical Tension: Sufficiency and Parsimony in QCA." *Sociological Methods & Research*, November 2019: 1–25. https://doi.org/10.1177/0049124119882456

Edelman, Marc, Carlos Oya, and Saturnino Borras. 2013. "Global Land Grabs: Historical Processes, Theoretical and Methodological Implications and Current Trajectories." *Third World Quarterly* 34: 1517–1531. https://doi.org/10.1080/01436597.2013.850190

Evans, Peter. 1995. *Embedded Autonomy: States and Industrial Transformation*. Princeton: Princeton University Press. https://doi.org/10.1515/9781400821723

Evans, Peter. 2010. "Constructing the 21st Century Developmental State: Potentialities and Pitfalls." In *Constructing a Democratic Developmental State in South Africa: Potentials and Challenges*, edited by Omano Edigheji, 37–58. Capetown: HSRC Press.

Falleti, Tulia G., and Julia Lynch. 2008. "From Process to Mechanism: Varieties of Disaggregation." *Qualitative Sociology* 31: 333–339. https://doi.org/10.1007/s11133-008-9102-4

Fiss, Peer C., Axel Marx, and Benoît Rihoux. 2014. "Comment: Getting QCA Right." *Sociological Methodology* 44 (1): 95–100. https://doi.org/10.1177/0081175014542079

Fitzpatrick, Patrick, Alberto Fonseca, and Mary Louise McAllister. 2011. "From the Whitehorse Mining Initiative Towards Sustainable Mining: Lessons Learned." *Journal of Cleaner Production* 19 (4): 376–384. https://doi.org/10.1016/j.jclepro.2010.10.013

Frank, Andre Gunder, and Barry K. Gills, eds. 1993. *The World System: Five Hundred Years or Five Thousand?* London: Routledge. https://doi.org/10.5195/jwsr.1995.52

References

Gerrits, Lasse, and Sofia Pagliarin. 2020. "Social and Causal Complexity in Qualitative Comparative Analysis (QCA): Strategies to Account for Emergence." *International Journal of Social Research Methodology*, 1–14. https://doi.org/10.1080/13645579.2020.1799636

Gerrits, Lasse, and Stefaan Verweij. 2018. *The Evaluation of Complex Infrastructure Projects: A Guide to Qualitative Comparative Analysis*. Cheltenham: Edward Elgar.

Giugni, Marco. 2004. *Social Protest and Policy Change: Ecology, Antinuclear, and Peace Movements in Comparative Perspective*. Lanham, MD: Rowman & Littlefield Publishers.

Giugni, Marco, and Maria Grasso. 2015. "Environmental Movements: Heterogeneity, Transformation, and Institutionalization." *Annual Review of Environment and Resources* 40: 337–361. https://doi.org/10.1146/annurev-environ-102014-021327

Giugni, Marco, and Sakura Yamasaki. 2009. "The Policy Impact of Social Movements: A Replication Through Qualitative Comparative Analysis." *Mobilization: An International Quarterly* 14 (4): 467–484. https://doi.org/10.17813/maiq.14.4.m2w21h55x5562r57

Guzmán, Tracey. 2013. *Native and National in Brazil: Indigeneity after Independence*. Chapel Hill, NC: The University of North Carolina Press. https://doi.org/10.5149/9781469602103_guzman

Haesebrouck, Tim, and Eva Thomann. 2021, forthcoming. "Introduction: Causation, Correctness, and Solution Types in Configurational Comparative Methods." *Quality and Quantity*.

Haslam, Paul Alexander, and Nasser Ary Tanimoune. 2016. "The Determinants of Social Conflict in the Latin American Mining Sector: New Evidence with Quantitative Data." *World Development* 78: 401–419. https://doi.org/10.1016/j.worlddev.2015.10.020

Hitchcock, Christopher. 2018. "Probabilistic Causation." In *The Stanford Encyclopedia of Philosophy*, edited by Edward N. Zalta. https://plato.stanford.edu/archives/fall2018/entries/causation-probabilistic/

Kahwati, Leila, and Heather Kane. 2019. *Qualitative Comparative Analysis in Mixed Methods Research and Evaluation*. Los Angeles, CA: Sage.

Kakar, Suhdir, and Katharina Kakar. 2007. *The Indians: Portrait of a People*. New Delhi: Penguin.

Karlsson, Bengt. 2011. *Unruly Hills: Nature and Nation in India's Northeast*. New Delhi: Orient BlackSwan.

King, Brayden. 2008. "A Political Mediation Model of Corporate Response to Social Movement Activism." *Administrative Science Quarterly* 53: 395–421. https://doi.org/10.2189/asqu.53.3.395

King, Brayden, and Sarah Soule. 2007. "Social Movements as Extra-institutional Entrepreneurs: The Effect of Protests on Stock Price Returns." *Administrative Science Quarterly* 52: 413–442. https://doi.org/10.2189/asqu.52.3.413

Kirsch, Stuart. 2013. *Mining Capitalism: The Relationship between Corporations and Their Critics*. Oakland, CA: University of California Press.

Krausova, A. (2020). "Latin American Social Movements: Bringing Strategy Back In." *Latin American Research Review* 55 (4): 839–849. http://doi.org/10.25222/larr.1398

References

Kröger, Markus. 2010. *The Politics of Pulp Investment and the Brazilian Landless Movement (MST)*. Acta Politica 39. Helsinki: University of Helsinki. http://urn.fi/URN:ISBN:978-952-10-6122-6

Kröger, Markus. 2011. "Promotion of Contentious Agency as a Rewarding Movement Strategy: Evidence from the MST-Paper Industry Conflicts in Brazil." *Journal of Peasant Studies* 38 (2): 435–458. https://doi.org/10.1080/03066150.2011.559016

Kröger, Markus. 2012. "Neo-Mercantilist Capitalism and Post-2008 Cleavages in Economic Decision-Making Power in Brazil." *Third World Quarterly* 33 (5): 887–901. https://doi.org/10.1080/01436597.2012.674703

Kröger, Markus. 2013. *Contentious Agency and Natural Resource Politics*. London: Routledge. https://doi.org/10.4324/9780203766736

Kröger, Markus. 2019. "O crescimento acelerado e o colapso do extrativismo do minério de ferro: o nexo Brasil-Índia-China." In *Desenvolvimento e transformações agrárias: BRICS, competição e cooperação no Sul Global*, edited by Sérgio Sauer, 307–24. São Paulo: Outras Expressões. http://hdl.handle.net/10138/305883

Kröger, Markus. 2020. *Iron Will: Global Extractivism and Mining Resistance in Brazil and India*. Ann Arbor, MI: University of Michigan Press. https://doi.org/10.3998/mpub.11533186

Kröger, Markus, and Rickard Lalander. 2016. "Ethnic-Territorial Rights and the Resource Extraction Boom in Latin America: Do Constitutions Matter?" *Third World Quarterly* 37 (4): 682–702. https://doi.org/10.1080/01436597.2015.1127154

Lazzarini, Sérgio G. 2011. *Capitalismo de laços: Os donos de Brasil e suas conexões*. Rio de Janeiro: Elsevier.

Li, Fabiana. 2015. *Unearthing Conflict: Corporate Mining, Activism, and Expertise in Peru*. Durham, NC: Duke University Press. https://doi.org/10.1215/9780822375869

Livingston, Julie. 2019. *Self-devouring Growth: A Planetary Parable as Told from Southern Africa*. Durham, NC: Duke University Press. https://doi.org/10.1215/9781478007005

Lu, Yao, and Ran Tao. 2017. "Organizational Structure and Collective Action: Lineage Networks, Semiautonomous Civic Associations, and Collective Resistance in Rural China." *American Journal of Sociology* 122 (6): 1726–1774. https://doi.org/10.1086/691346

Luders, Joseph. 2010. *The Civil Rights Movement and the Logic of Social Change*. Cambridge: Cambridge University Press. https://doi.org/10.1017/CBO9780511817120

MacKay, Joseph, and Jamie Levin. 2015. "Hanging Out in International Politics: Two Kinds of Explanatory Political Ethnography for IR." *International Studies Review* 17: 163–188. https://doi.org/10.1111/misr.12208

Marcus, George. 1995. "Ethnography in/of the World System: The Emergence of Multi-Sited Ethnography." *Annual Review of Anthropology* 24: 95–117. https://doi.org/10.1146/annurev.an.24.100195.000523

Marx, Axel, and Adrian Dușa. 2011. "Crisp-Set Qualitative Comparative Analysis (csQCA), Contradictions and Consistency Benchmarks for Model Specification."

Methodological Innovations Online 6 (2): 103–148. https://doi.org/10.4256/mio.2010.0037

McAdam, Doug, and Hilary Boudet. 2012. *Putting Social Movements in Their Place: Explaining Opposition to Energy Projects in the United States, 2000–2005*. New York: Cambridge University Press. https://doi.org/10.1017/CBO9781139105811

McAdam, Doug, Hilary Boudet, Jennifer Davis, Ryan Orr, W. Richard Scott, and Raymond E. Levitt. 2010. "'Site Fights': Explaining Opposition to Pipeline Projects in the Developing World." *Sociological Forum* 25: 401–427. https://doi.org/10.1111/j.1573-7861.2010.01189.x

McAdam, Doug, Sidney Tarrow, and Charles Tilly. 2001. *Dynamics of Contention*. Cambridge: Cambridge University Press. https://doi.org/10.1017/CBO9780511805431

McAdam, Doug, Sidney Tarrow, and Charles Tilly. 2008. "Methods for Measuring Mechanisms of Contention." *Qualitative Sociology* 31: 307–331. https://doi.org/10.1007/s11133-008-9100-6

McMichael, Philip. 1992. "Rethinking Comparative Analysis in a Post-Developmental Context." *International Social Science Journal* 133: 351–365.

McMichael, Philip. 2000. "World-Systems Analysis, Globalization, and Incorporated Comparison." *Journal of World-Systems Research* 6 (3): 68–99. https://doi.org/10.5195/jwsr.2000.192

Mello, Patrick. 2021, forthcoming. *Qualitative Comparative Analysis: Research Design and Application*. Washington, DC: Georgetown University Press.

Mies, Maria, and Vandana Shiva. 2014. *Ecofeminism*. London: Zed Books.

Mitchell, Timothy. 2011. *Carbon Democracy: Political Power in the Age of Oil*. London: Verso.

Moore, Jason W. 2015. *Capitalism in the Web of Life: Ecology and the Accumulation of Capital*. London: Verso Books.

Moreno, Camila. 2015. *O Brasil Made in China: Para pensar as reconfigurações do capitalismo contemporâneo*. São Paulo: Fundação Rosa Luxemburgo.

Nugent, Jeffrey, and James Robinson. 2010. "Are Factor Endowments Fate?" *Revista de Historia Economica/Journal of Iberian and Latin American Economic History* 28: 45–82. https://doi.org/10.1017/S0212610909990048

Olsen, Wendy. 2014. "Comment: The Usefulness of QCA Under Realist Assumptions." *Sociological Methodology* 44 (1): 101–107. https://doi.org/10.1177/0081175014542080

Omvedt, Gail. 2011. *Understanding Caste: From Buddha to Ambedkar and Beyond*, 2nd Edition. Hyderabad: Orient Blackswan.

Özkaynak, Begüm, Beatriz Rodriguez-Labajos, Cem İ. Aydın, Ivonne Yanez, and Claudio Garibay. 2015. "Towards Environmental Justice Success in Mining Conflicts: An Empirical Investigation." *EJOLT Report No. 14*. 96p. www.ejolt.org/2015/04/towards-environmental-justice-success-mining-conflicts/

Prates, Clarissa Godinho. 2017. *Efeitos derrame da mineração, violências cotidianas e resistências em Conceição do Mato Dentro-MG*. Master thesis, UFMG. https://repositorio.ufmg.br/bitstream/1843/NCAP-AVDK4X/1/clarissa_disserta__o_edit_2_3_edi__o.pdf

References

Ragin, Charles. 1987. *The Comparative Method: Moving Beyond Qualitative and Quantitative Strategies*. Berkeley, CA: University of California Press.

Ragin, Charles. 2014. "Comment: Lucas and Szatrowski in Critical Perspective." *Sociological Methodology* 44 (1): 80–94. https://doi.org/10.1177/0081175014542081

Ragin, Charles. 2019. "Case-oriented Research and the Study of Social Action." In *Rational Choice Theory and Large-scale Data Analysis*, edited by Hans-Peter Blossfeld and Gerald Prein, 158–168. New York: Routledge. https://doi.org/10.4324/9780429303753

Ragin, Charles, and Sarah Strand. 2008. "Using Qualitative Comparative Analysis to Study Causal Order: Comment on Caren and Panofsky (2005)." *Sociological Methods & Research* 36: 431–441. https://doi.org/10.1177/0049124107313903

Rajak, Dinah. 2011. *In Good Company: An Anatomy of Corporate Social Responsibility*. Stanford, CA: Stanford University Press. https://doi.org/10.1515/9780804781619

Rihoux, Benoît. 2008. "Case-Oriented Configurational Research: Qualitative Comparative Analysis (QCA), Fuzzy Sets, and Related Techniques." In *The Oxford Handbook of Political Methodology*, edited by Janet Box-Steffensmeier et al., 722–736. Oxford: Oxford University Press. https://doi.org/10.1093/oxfordhb/9780199286546.001.0001

Rihoux, Benoît. 2016. "Configurational Comparative Methods (QCA and Fuzzy Sets): Complex Causation in Cross-case Analysis." In *Handbook of Research Methods and Applications in Political Science*, edited by Hans Keman and Jaap J. Woldendorp, 383–400. Northampton, MA: Edward Elgar Publishing. https://doi.org/10.4337/9781784710828

Rihoux, Benoît. 2020. "Qualitative Comparative Analysis: Discovering Core Combinations of Conditions in Political Decision Making." In *Oxford Research Encyclopedia of Politics*. Oxford: Oxford University Press. https://doi.org/10.1093/acrefore/9780190228637.013.1342

Rihoux, Benoît, Priscilla Álamos Concha, and Bojana Lobe. 2021, forthcoming. "Qualitative Comparative Analysis (QCA): An Integrative Approach Suited for Diverse Mixed Methods and Multimethod Research Strategies." In *Routledge Reviewer's Guide to Mixed Methods Analysis*, edited by Tony Onwuegbuzie and Burke Johnson. Oxon and London: Routledge.

Rihoux, Benoît, and Gisèle De Meur. 2009. "Crisp-Set Qualitative Comparative Analysis (csQCA)." In *Configurational Comparative Methods: Qualitative Comparative Analysis (QCA) and Related Techniques*, edited by Benoît Rihoux and Charles C. Ragin, 33–68. Applied Social Research Methods. Thousand Oaks, CA: SAGE Publications. https://doi.org/10.4135/9781452226569

Rihoux, Benoît, and Bojana Lobe. 2009. "The Case for Qualitative Comparative Analysis (QCA): Adding Leverage for Thick Cross-case Comparison." In *The SAGE Handbook of Case-Based Methods*, edited by David Byrne and Charles Ragin, 222–242. Thousand Oaks, CA: SAGE Publications Ltd. https://doi.org/10.4135/9781446249413.n13

Rihoux, Benoit, and Charles Ragin, eds. 2009. *Configurational Comparative Methods: Qualitative Comparative Analysis (QCA) and Related Techniques*. Thousand Oaks, CA: SAGE Publications. https://doi.org/10.4135/9781452226569

References

Rihoux, Benoît, Charles Ragin, Sakura Yamasaki, and Damien Bol. 2009. "Conclusions—The Way(s) Ahead." In *Configurational Comparative Methods: Qualitative Comparative Analysis (QCA) and Related Techniques*, edited by Benoît Rihoux and Charles C. Ragin, 167–178. Thousand Oaks, CA: SAGE Publications, Inc. https://doi.org/10.4135/9781452226569.n8

Santos, Ana Flávia Moreira, Luciana da Silva Sales Ferreira, and Vinicius Villela Penna. 2017. "Impactos Supostos, Violências Reais: A Construção da Legalidade na Implantação do Projeto Minas-Rio." *Vibrant: Virtual Brazilian Anthropology* 14 (2): 1–25. http://doi.org/10.1590/1809-43412017v14n2p159

Schatz, Edward, ed. 2009. *Political Ethnography: What Immersion Contributes to the Study of Power*. Chicago: University of Chicago Press.

Schneider, Carsten Q., and Ingo Rohlfing. 2013. "Combining QCA and Process Tracing in Set-theoretic Multi-method Research." *Sociological Methods & Research* 42 (4): 559–597. https://doi.org/10.1177/0049124113481341

Scott, James C. 2008. *Weapons of the Weak: Everyday Forms of Peasant Resistance*. New Haven and London: Yale University Press. https://hdl.handle.net/2027/heb.02471

Sherman, Daniel. 2011. "Critical Mechanisms for Critical Masses: Exploring Variation in Opposition to Low-level Radioactive Waste Site Proposals." *Mobilization* 16 (1): 81–100. https://doi.org/10.17813/maiq.16.1.gt7617043n132422

Small, Mario Luis. 2013. "Causal Thinking and Ethnographic Research." *American Journal of Sociology* 119 (3): 597–601. https://doi.org/10.1086/675893

Snow, David A., Robert D. Benford, Holly J. McCammon, Lyndi Hewitt, and Scott Fitzgerald. 2014. "The Emergence, Development, and Future of the Framing Perspective: 25+ Years since 'Frame Alignment'." *Mobilization* 19 (1): 23–45. https://doi.org/10.17813/maiq.19.1.x74278226830m69l

Solingen, Etel, and Peter Gourevitch. 2017. "Domestic Coalitions: International Sources and Effect." Published in *Oxford Research Encyclopedia of Empirical International Relations Theory*, edited by William R. Thompson. Oxford: Oxford University Press. https://doi.org/10.1093/acrefore/9780190228637.013.353

Soule, Sarah. 2009. *Contention and Corporate Social Responsibility*. Cambridge: Cambridge University Press. https://doi.org/10.1017/CBO9780511804359

Suh, Doowon. 2012. "Intricacies of Social Movement Outcome Research and Beyond: 'How Can You Tell' Social Movements Prompt Changes?" *Sociological Research Online* 17 (4): 92–102. https://doi.org/10.5153/sro.2757

Tavory, Iddo, and Stefan Timmermans. 2013. "A Pragmatist Approach to Causality in Ethnography." *American Journal of Sociology* 119 (3): 682–714. https://doi.org/10.1086/675891

Thiem, Alrik, and Adrian Duşa. 2013. *Qualitative Comparative Analysis with R: A User's Guide*. New York: Springer. https://doi.org/10.1007/978-1-4614-4584-5

Thomann, Eva, and Martino Maggetti. 2020. "Designing Research with Qualitative Comparative Analysis (QCA): Approaches, Challenges, and Tools." *Sociological Methods & Research* 49 (2): 356–386. https://doi.org/10.1177/0049124117729700

Vaisey, Stephen. 2014. "Comment: QCA Works—When Used with Care." *Sociological Methodology* 44 (1): 108–112. https://doi.org/10.1177/0081175014542083

Vale. 2012. *Annual Report 2011.* Accessed May 24, 2012 www.vale.com.br/en-us/investidores/relatorios-anuais-e-de-sustentabilidade/2011/Documents/20F_2011_i.pdf

Vasi, Ian. 2009. "Social Movements and Industry Development: The Environmental Movement's Impact on the Wind Energy Industry." *Mobilization* 14: 315–336. https://doi.org/10.17813/maiq.14.3.j534128155107051

Vélez-Torres, Irene. 2014. "Governmental Extractivism in Colombia: Legislation, Securitization and the Local Settings of Mining Control." *Political Geography* 38: 68–78. https://doi.org/10.1016/j.polgeo.2013.11.008

Wagemann, C. 2014. "Qualitative Comparative Analysis (QCA): What It Is, What It Does, and How It Works." In *Methodological Practices in Social Movement Research*, edited by Donatella della Porta, 43–66. Oxford: Oxford University Press. https://doi.org/10.1093/acprof:oso/9780198719571.001.0001

Wallerstein, Immanuel. 1974. *The Modern World-system: Capitalist Agriculture and the Origins of the European World Economy in the Sixteenth Century.* New York: Academic Press.

Wallerstein, Immanuel. 1998. *Utopistics: Or, Historical Choices of the Twenty-first Century.* New York: The New Press.

Watts, Michael. 2004. "Resource Curse? Governmentality, Oil and Power in the Niger Delta, Nigeria." *Geopolitics* 9 (1): 50–80. https://doi.org/10.1080/14650040412331307832

Wilkinson, Steven I. 2013. "Communal and Caste Politics and Conflicts in India." In *Routledge Handbook of South Asian Politics*, edited by Paul R. Brass, 262–273. London: Routledge. https://doi.org/10.4324/9780203878187

Zhouri, Andréa, and Norma Valencio, eds. 2014. *Formas de Matar, de Morrer e de Resistir: Limites da Resolução Negociada de Conflitos Ambientais (Forms to Kill, to Die and to Resist: Limits of Negotiated Resolution of Environmental Conflicts).* Belo Horizonte: Editora UFMG.

Zonta, M., and C. Trocate. 2016. *A questão mineral no Brasil—vol. 2: Antes fosse mais leve a carga: reflexões sobre o desastre da Samarco/ Vale/BHP Billiton.* Marabá: Editorial iGuana.

Index

agency 35, 45, 47, 75; armed resistance 46, 61, 67; armed revolutionary 36, 40, **56**, 58, 67–69, 74–75, 79; extractive 21–**22**, 106; political 37; *see also* corporate agency
algorithm 11, 14, 25, 84, 118; algorithmizing 48n2
Anglo American 48n4, **52**, 56, 95–96, 100, 110
armed resistance 7, 37, 40, 65, 69–70, 103, 110

binary logic *see* Boolean logic
Boolean logic 4–5, 8n1, 16, 37–38, 46, 59, 70, 77, 84, 121, 123; minimization 2
bounded area of impact 21

case selection 38–39
causal analysis 8n1, 16, 18, 114
causal condition complexes 7, 11, 13–15, 36, 44, 54, 65, 74, 113, 122–123
causal conditions 21, 24, 33–35, 45–48n2, 79, 84, 88, 91–93n6, 105, 117–118; change 18; complex 69–70, 113–114; elimination of 2, 96; large number of 12, 40, 120–122; necessary and sufficient 13–14, 16, 40, 54, 81–82, 86; not sufficient 64; potential 19; *see also* causal condition complexes; explanatory factors
causality 4, 16, 21, 31n1, 35, 44
causal "paths" 2, 5, 15–16, 39, 47–48, 67, 118

complex: interactions 6, 33, 95, 101
complex analysis 120
complex contextual factors 70
composition of capital 47
concrete cases 6
condensed analysis 48, 94; *see also* QCA tables
configurational comparison techniques 3
constraints of QCA 123; *see also* binary logic; Boolean logic
contradictory configurations 13, 59–60, 62, 82, 120n3
corporate agency 44–45, 56–57, 67, 78–79, 81, 86, 94, 123; differences 40, 47, 70, **72**, 109; third parties 105–106; the state 109–113
corporate counter tactics 47, **72**, 79, **80**, 95–96, 100
corporate social responsibility **22–23**, 44, **56**, 81, 106, 111, 113
corporations: BHP Billiton 106, 110; KIOCL Limited 49n6, **51–52**; Jindal **51–52**, 106; POSCO **51–52**, 106, 115–116nn12–13; SAIL Corporation 49n6, **51–52**, 106; Tata **51–52**, 106, 115–116n13; Vedanta 106; *see also* Anglo American; Vale
Crisp-set QCA (csQCA) 4–6, 14–18, 35, 37–38, 100, 121; constraint of 123; systematic 46; truth tables 69, 72, 89
Cronqvist, Lasse 13, 83, 118; *see also* Excel tool
cross-contextual comparison 36, 120–121
cross-continental analysis 39

Index 135

database 6, 37, 39, 44–45, 84–85, 93n6, 120nn3–4, 121; analysis of 48; complex 61–62, 117, 123; design 15, 19; existing 28; interview 30; real world 13
data calibration 33
dataset: large-n 124; medium-n 9, 12, 38, 124; small-n 9, 124
disaggregation 21, **22**

economic outcome 19, 35–36, 40, 44, 54, 62, 67, 69, 102
electoral politics **22**, **56**, 64, 99
embedded autonomy 43
embedding the state **22–23**, 41, 43, 48n3, **56**, 58, 63–65, 75, 82, 99; tactics 86, 111
ethnic relations 70, 86, 94–95, 101–105, 114n3, 123
Excel tool 13, 60, 72–73, 82–84, 86, 118
explanatory factors 2, 4, 6, 10–12, 31n1, 37, 45, 70; key 39
extractivism **22**, 32n3, 37, 64, 73–74, 81, 84, 95, 101–102, 105–108; resistance to 24, 40, 44, 60, 69

factors: contingency 12, 37, 41, 45–46, 49, 73, 94, 113–114; contextual 46, 48, 59, 70–**71**, 101
field research 3, 16, 19, 33–36, 38, 92, 99, 101, 122; assistants 31; ethnographic 6–7, 12, 120n2, 124; observations 45–46, 115n6; skills 24–26, 30
five key strategies 41, 45, 67, 86, 91
fuzzy: fsQCA 4–5, 17, 32n2, 101, 121; logic 9, 14, 89

Galton's problem 18
generalizable conclusion 67
geographic factor 40, 45, **72**, 77

heuristic tools 37, 41, 57
Hume, David 2, 8n1

institutional politics **22**, 42, **56**, 58, 64
invented counterfactuals 11
investment politics 17–18, 22, 24, 35–38, 48n4, 65, 88, 92, 95, 114n3; future studies of 101, 121; outcomes 6, 42–43, 59, 70, 86, 106

judicial politics **22**, 42–43, **56**, 62, 64

key factors 41, 62–65, 101; *see also* explanatory factors

logical remainders 11–13, **83**–84, 118

mapping 20, 28
mechanism based explanations 17, 40
methodological tactics 120
minimal causal combination 4
minimal formula 5, 18, 31n1, 59, 70, 88–89, 120nn2–4, 122; exercise 81–83, 86, 91
multi-sited ethnography 3, 12–15, 27, 30, 72, 86
multi-sited political ethnography 14, 19, 24, 119, 121
multi-value QCA (mvQCA) 4, 10, 14, 100, 121

necessary causal conditions 69, 82, 122
networking (with other resistance groups) **22**, 39, 41–42, **56**, 63, 75, 82, 99
nonobserved cases 5, 38, 84, 91, 121

outcome factors 11, 96

parsimonious 18, 46; explanations 12–13, 32n1, 59, 81, 86–88, 118–120; solution 11–13, 84, 118–119
peaceful movements 40; protest 41, 70, 103; radical contention 86; resistance 40, 58, 61, 65–**67**, 69, 91; setting 13, 61, 74
political ethnography 12, 15, 24
political outcomes 35–37, 44, **55–57**, 61, 69, 73–74, 77–78, 92
Popper, Karl 2, 8n1
positionality 36
positivist 2
probabilistic analysis 5, 86, 120, 122
process-tracing 4–5, 10

QCA tables 5, 13–14, 28, 37, 41, 44, 54, 62, 64, 69, 89, 92

Ragin, Charles 2, 32n2, 34, 118
regression analysis 17
relational mechanisms 18

set-theoretic approach 11
snowball method 15, 122
social movements 16–17, 36, 42–43, 60, 70, 75, 79, 82; analysis of 19, 35, 121; lack of 29
synchronous cases 18
systematic analysis 4, 19, 28, 47

temporal 105; analysis 18, 91, 95; data 78, 82; differences 7; QCA 61–62, 91
text-based data collection 6
theoretical-empirical findings 44–45
third-party roles 47, **72**

transparency 16–17, 21, 70, 81, 89, 119
transparent recalibration 89
triangulation 16, 28, 38, 46, 92, 100, 117; data 5, 30; researcher-analysis 31, 88, 99; theoretical 31
truth table 5, 14, 16, 37, 39, 59, 61, 72, 81–**87**, 89, 111; analysis 69–70, 91, 94, 114, 123
type of target 47, **72**, 74

Vale **23**, 28–29, 49n6, **52–53**, 79, 106, 110, 112–113, 116n17; resistance 42, 56–57, 59, 62
variable-based regression analysis 17
variables: dependent 2, 36, 39, 44, 70; static 17

world-political ethnography 15